Family Cemeteries
and
Grave Sites
in
Harford County, Maryland

Henry C. Peden Jr.

Colonial Roots
Millsboro, Delaware
2016

Colonial
Roots

Helping You Grow Your Family Tree

ISBN 978-1-68034-144-7

Cover photo: Priestford Cemetery by Jack L. Shagena Jr., 2010

CONTENTS

INTRODUCTION

Over the years, tombstones in family cemeteries have been copied by many Harford County researchers. Some of their lists were donated to the Historical Society of Harford County and those who have contributed information include, but are not limited to, George W. Archer, Doris P. Barben, Margaret S. Bishop, Reggie Bishop, Charmaine Brankowitz, Mary Bristow, Frederick L. Cobourn, Patricia Czerniewski, Sally Hesson, John D. Hiteshew, Sr., William D. Hiteshew, Jr., Joseph C. Hopkins, John C. Houck, Joseph Lee Hughes, Leonard Laylon, Jon Harlan Livezey, Dorothy E. O'Donnell, Jennette Parker, Henry C. Peden, Jr., Carol Porter, Jack L. Shagena, Jr., Christopher T. Smithson, Harry W. Spraker, Gertrude J. Stephens and James T. Wollon, Jr.

It is fortunate indeed that the aforementioned copyists did their duty in preserving this information because many tombstones have since disappeared. Some family cemeteries now rest in restricted areas of the Aberdeen Proving Ground. We are again fortunate that photographs of those tombstones were taken by the U. S. Government in 1999 and a copy of their work is at the Historical Society of Harford County.

In addition, burial information has been gleaned from extant newspapers, death certificates, some church records, family histories and local histories. Annotations have also been inserted [in brackets] within the text in an effort to further identify those buried here. Any researchers who have more information about old family cemeteries should submit their material for preservation at the Historical Society of Harford County, 143 N. Main Street, Bel Air, MD 21014.

Henry C. Peden, Jr.
April 15, 2016

[this page intentionally blank]

FAMILY CEMETERIES AND GRAVE SITES IN HARFORD COUNTY, MARYLAND

AMOS CEMETERY

This cemetery is located on "Uphill Farm" at 2131 Baldwin Mill Road between Upper Cross Roads and Madonna in northwestern Harford County. Some information had been provided by Dorothy E. O'Donnell of Jarrettsville, Maryland in 2010 via Leonard Laylon, Cemetery Records Chairman at the Historical Society of Harford County. *Children of Mt. Soma*, by Gertrude J. Stephens (1992), p. 20, stated there are also several children buried here. [Information in brackets added below by Henry C. Peden, Jr. between 2011-2015.]

Amos, Robert Sr., died 10 Oct 1818 in his 77th year
[Robert rendered patriotic service in the Revolutionary War.]

Amos, Martha, consort of Robert Amos, Sr., died 10 Apr 1832 in her 83rd year

Amos, Elizabeth, wife of Robert (her marker is missing)

Amos, Robert Jr., 6 May 1771 – 14 Oct 1826
[Robert was a corporal in the militia in the War of 1812.]

McComas, Aquilla, died 5 Mar 1825 in his 52nd year, leaving a wife and 2 children
[Aquilla was a lieutenant in the militia in the War of 1812.]

McComas, Martha Amos, wife of Aquilla (marker missing)
[*The Amos Family Genealogy*, by Mrs. Fred L. Bull (1938), states Martha McComas was born in 1749 and died in 1832.]

Amoss, Daniel, 13 Oct 1768 – 5 Mar 1854
[Daniel was a private in the militia in the War of 1812.]

Amoss, Sarah, wife of Daniel, 7 Oct 1771 – 14 Aug 1858

BARNES – BAILEY CEMETERY
(BAYVIEW or COEN'S HILL CEMETERY)

This cemetery on Earlton Road is about two miles west of Evans Corner, north of Chapel Road and near to Havre de Grace. It was incorporated as "Bayview Cemetery" in 1892. When the tombstones were copied circa 1950-1960 an unidentified copyist noted that the cemetery is "located on Carlisle property, now owned by a Mr. Frazier. Cemetery not part of farm retained by family – land deeded as cemetery, 1867. First interment in 1765. First Barnes owner was Gregory Barnes, Sr. Fenced size of cemetery, 140' x 160', board fence. Cemetery kept cleaned, 4 pine trees stand in enclosure, many grey stones without marks. Sunken graves were filled. Apparently last burial was that of Clifford Colfax Barnes, buried March 20, 1945. No stones to indicate early burial of 1765 (first interment)." In 2011 Christopher T. Smithson, of Darlington, MD, noted that William Colfax Barnes died in 1986, his wife Betsy Boyd Barnes died in 2005 and they are buried here. Madilyn Crane, of Austin, TX, in 2012, stated Bay View Cemetery was better known as Coen's Hill. [Information in brackets below was added by Henry C. Peden, Jr. in 2015.]

Barnes, Hannah Elizabeth Hughes, 1876-1919, wife of Clifford Barnes

Barnes, Clifford Colfax, 1868 – 17 Mar 1945

Barnes, Mary Frances, wife of Richard A., died 17 Dec 1887, age 57

Barnes, Richard Amos, 12 Feb 1834 – 31 May 1913, husband of Mary Frances Noble and Mary V. Parker

Barnes, Richard Randolph, 25 Feb 1896 – 6 Aug 1896, son of Wilmer L. and Ellen R.

Treadway, Ellen Barnes, 19 Mar 1860 – 3 Oct 1906

Tredway [Treadway], Sarah A., 6 Dec 1832 – 25 Aug 1901, wife of Aquila E. Tredway

Tredway [Treadway], Aquila E., 4 Apr 1826 – 9 Nov 1887

Barnes, Sarah, 23 Aug 1873, age 81, wife of Mordecai G

Barnes, Mordecai G. [Gilbert], died 30 Apr 1866, age 75

Barnes, Winston, 24 Jul 1820 – 6 Nov 1863

Barnes, Richard, 27 Mar 1822 – 20 Mar 1893

Barnes, Mary J. [Jane], 3 Oct 1822 – 6 Jul 1901, wife of Richard Barnes

Bailey, Ezra, died 20 Oct 1866, age 63

Barnes, F. [Frances] Cordelia, 21 Jul 1843 – 28 Feb 1906

Barnes, Mary E., 29 Sep 1838 – 31 Aug 1918

Barnes, William H. [Henry], 3 Nov 1840 – 21 Jul 1928

Barnes, Richard, 24 Jan 1805 – 10 Sep 1849

Barnes, Susanna, 4 Jun 1808 – 27 Oct 1892, wife of Richard

Barnes, Mary, born 16 Apr 1835, died same year, daughter of Richard and Susanna Barnes [*Barnes-Bailey Genealogy*, by Walter D. Barnes (1939), stated she died 17 Jul 1835.]

Barnes, W. [William] Harrison, 21 Feb 1837 – 19 Aug 1836, son of Richard and Susanna Barnes

Carsins, James, died 13 Nov 1878, age 28 years, 5 months and 20 days, son of William and Martha Carsins

Carsins, George, died 27 Jul 1849, age 2 months and 9 days, son of William and Martha Carsins

Carsins, James, 18 Dec 1824 – 20 Jun 1848, son of John and Ann Carsins

Carsins, George, 23 Jan 1834 – 20 Oct 1849, son of John and Ann Carsins

Carsins, Jane, 3 Jun 1828 – 4 Mar 1832, daughter of John and Ann Carsins

Carsins, Ann, died 25 Jan 1879, age 80 years, 11 months and 9 days, wife of John Carsins

Carsins, John, 18 Feb 1795 – 20 Oct 1838

Barnes, William, 26 Mar 1804 – 18 Jun 1872

Barnes, Elizabeth, 8 Sep 1775-28 Apr 1859, wife of Gregory

Barnes, Gregory Jr., 17 Dec 1765 – 26 Nov 1846

Bailey, Avarilla, died Mar 1847, age 88

Bailey, Joshua, died Dec 1842, age 94

Brown stone marked G. B. 1846

Brown stone marked S. B. 1849

Brown stone marked J. M. B. 1847

Bailey, Asael, 27 Aug 1778 – 21 Sep 1825

Bailey, Mary, 7 Sep 1787 – 3 Sep 1828

Bailey, James H., 10 May 1820 – 19 Jul 1883

Bailey, Charles Lewis, 14 Nov 1824 – 2 Jun 1895

Bailey, Elizabeth, 10 Dec 1808 – 26 Feb 1854

Coen, Nancy, Mrs., died 7 Jun 1866, age 67

Coen, John, died 2 Feb 1871, age 79

Coen, Elizabeth, 23 Nov 1791 – 28 Mar 1818, wife of John

Fletcher, Albert, 3 Mar 1837 – 23 Nov 1837

Fletcher, Samuel, 26 Jun 1788 – 12 Feb 1855

Fletcher, Mary, died 27 Apr 1884, age 85, wife of Samuel

Maxwell, Amos, 20 Jan 1804 – 2 May 1888

Maxwell, Elizabeth, 29 May 1788 – 9 Mar 1853, wife of Amos Maxwell

Barnes, Elizabeth, died 18 Apr 1832, age 93, wife of Gregory Barnes, Sr.

Barnes, Gregory Sr., died 26 Mar 1808, age 74

Bailey, Rachel, died 27 Apr 1850, age 86 years, 1 month and 5 days

Bailey, Evan, 30 Jul 1803 – 7 Jul 1875

Bailey, Martha, 4 Feb 1804 – 25 Nov 1882, wife of Aquila

Bailey, Aquila, 13 Sep 1806 – 10 Mar 1888

Coen, Henry C., died 29 Dec 1869, age 36

Coen, Sarah Ann, 19 Sep 1826 – 16 Jul 1877

Barnes, John, 10 Apr 1783 [1788?] – 23 Mar 1843

Brown stone marked M. B. – no dates [probably Mary Barnes, died 1815]

Brown stone marked F. B. – no dates [probably Ford Barnes, died 1798]

Barnes, Richard Sr., died 29 Nov 1830, age 68

Barnes, Sarah, died 13 Feb 1811, age 49, wife of Richard Barnes, Sr.

Barnes, William Colfax, 3 May 1908 – 1986

Barnes, Betsy Boyd, died 2005, wife of William Colfax Barnes

Thompson, Sarah B., 5 Jan 1832 – 3 Dec 1916 [neé Barnes, wife of John C. Thompson; no marker, but her death certificate states she was buried in the family burying ground near Webster.]

BAYVIEW CEMETERY
(see Barnes-Bailey Cemetery)

BIGGS GRAVE SITE

Death certificate of Baby Boy Biggs, son of Mary Elizabeth Biggs and grandson of James D. Biggs, indicates the infant was stillborn on 11 Apr 1948 and was buried in woods by his grandfather near the shack where they lived on the Livezey Farm, Rural Aberdeen (Mt. Royal Avenue). It is interesting to note that on the death certificate it stated "Mother swears there was no father!!!" [sic]

BOND CEMETERY

In 1976 an unidentified copyist stated, "These items were deposited with other building materials by the owner of the property on which the cemetery stood on the land of James T. Wollon, Jr. at Rock Run. The cemetery was (is) on the land of J. Rayman, on Toll Gate Road, south of U. S. Route #1, near Bel Air." [Historical Society of Harford County file]

Complete stone: In memory of Nicholas M. Bond, 23 May 1797 – 15 Apr 1866
Small fragment: r 16th [sic]
Part of footstone: R. A. – (last initial missing)

Circa 2005 it was determined by the late Margaret S. Bishop that Eliza Carnan Holland, wife of Robert W. Holland, died 9 Apr 1878 and was buried here, but there is no marker.

BROWN – COLLINS CEMETERY

Identified as Aberdeen Proving Ground Private Cemetery P-2 by the U. S. Government, this cemetery is located near the intersection of Palmer Road and an unidentified road west of Michaelsville Road. See the binders of *Silent Sentinels of Aberdeen Proving Ground* (1999) at the Historical Society of

Harford County in Bel Air, Maryland for tombstone images and further cemetery details. [Information in brackets was added by Henry C. Peden, Jr. in 2015. By all indications this was an African American cemetery. An unidentified copyist in 1958 mentioned several, but not all, of these stones.]

Reed, Lillie Eliza Jane, died 25 Feb 1904, age 21 [sic] years, 2 months and 23 days [Death certificate stated she was a single African American and died at age 24.]

Hill, Mary J., died 19 Jan 1899, age 20, wife of David J. Hill

Hill, David J., died 19 Jul 1900, age 30 [Death certificate stated David Hill was an African American and a widower.]

York, John W., died 7 Jan 1892, age 63

Stewart, John F., died 9 Mar 1902 in his 47th year

Smith, Daniel, died 18 Nov 1906, age 73

Flint, Julia A., age 13 (no dates)

Harris, Elizabeth, 9 May 1848 – 2 Sep 1903, daughter of John and Milcah Harris

Brown, William, 30 Jun 1835 – 13 Nov 1855

Dennison, Araminta, 22 Apr 1824 – 3 Dec 1870

Dennison, Lydia E., died 8 Aug 1889, age 73 [Unidentified copyist in 1958 listed this marker, but it was not included in the list prepared by the U. S. Government in 1999]

Hollingsworth, Eliza, died 22 Mar 1889, age 66

Harris, Henry, 12 Sep 1842 – 12 Jun 1890

Harris, Littleton R. E., 20 Feb 1871 – 15 Sep 1896

Ringgold, John H., died 15 Feb 1885 in his 72nd year

Hollingsworth, W. (?), 27 May 1825 – 2 Feb 1892 [as listed by the government in 1999]

Hollingsworth, Henry, died 2 Feb 1872, age 47 [as listed by unknown copyist in 1958]

Loveday, Harriet, died 26 Apr 1886, age 70 (marker erected by her children)

Boyer, Harriet, died 11 Oct 1877, age 68 [Unidentified copyist on 18 Sep 1958 listed this marker as 11 Dec 1877, age 68, but the list prepared by the U. S. Government in 1999 gave the date as 11 Oct 1877, age 68.]

Collins, Mary, died 25 Oct 1830, age 35, wife of Len Collins

Footstone: M. L.

Footstone: H. B.

Stansbury, Anna Maria, 1817 – 25 Jul 1876

Collins, Levin, died 22 Jan 1913, age 70
[Death certificate stated Leven H. Collins was an African American, birth date unknown, possibly 70 years old, and he was buried in Union Chapel Cemetery.]

Tildon, Henry E., 15 Oct 1842 – 10 Mar 1901
[Death certificate stated he was an African American, born 15 Oct 1841.]

Warfield, Annie, died 9 Feb 1893, age 48 [Unidentified copyist on 18 Sep 1958 listed this marker, but it was not included in the list prepared by the U. S. Government in 1999; however, they did list this footstone: A. M. W.]

BROWNE GRAVE SITE
(see Oakington Grave Site)

CAIN GRAVE SITE

On 30 May 1890 *The Harford Democrat* reported "Dr. Geo. W. Archer has collected and removed from the old burying ground at Priestford ---- [illegible] --- Harford Historical Society, the fragments of an old tombstone from the grave of James Cain who, according to the inscription, was born 'on ye 9th day of March, in ye year of God 1752' and departed this life in 1797. It is thought to be the oldest tombstone in the county." [Ed. Note: James Cain was a private in Capt. John Archer's Company in 1775. His tombstone fragments no longer exist, but his grave is somewhere on Deer Creek.]

CHAUNCEY CEMETERY

Identified as Aberdeen Proving Ground Private Cemetery P-7 by the U. S. Government, this cemetery is located on Abbey Point Road near Redman Cove. See the binders of *Silent Sentinels of Aberdeen Proving Ground* (1999) at the Historical Society of Harford County in Bel Air, Maryland for tombstone images and cemetery details. [Information in brackets below was added by Henry C. Peden, Jr. in 2015.]

Cole, Joseph, died 18 Sep 1800, age 27 years and 7 months

Chauncey, George, died 29 Dec 1801, age 63
[He was a private in the militia in the Revolutionary War.]

Chauncey, Mary, died 1 Jul 1798, age 51

Chauncey, James M., died 30 Apr 1813 (marker not found)

CHESNEY CEMETERY

This cemetery was once located on Rock Run Road on a farm owned by Carroll Craig. It measured about 25' x 40' and was close to the road by a fence. It has also been described as being on the Old Hopkins Farm near the Old Camp Ground, but there are no markers today. The two tombstones below were removed years ago and placed in an outbuilding on Little Pines Farm in Darlington, according to researcher Christopher T. Smithson who has pictures of them. [Information in brackets below was added by Henry C. Peden, Jr. in 2016.]

Chesney, William, born in Cecil County, 27 Aug 1756, died 29 May 1840 [William Chesney took the Oath of Allegiance in Cecil County in 1778.]

Chesney, Mary, consort of William, born in Cecil County, 1758, died 3 Jan 1830

CHRISTY GRAVE SITE

Death certificate stated there was the premature delivery of a boy about eight months old on 24 Oct 1913, the unnamed son of William Christy and Martha Boulden who lived near Aberdeen, and the infant was buried by his father on the farm near their house.

CLARK CEMETERY

In an article titled "Letter from Castleton" in *The Aegis & Intelligencer* on 9 May 1879, it stated the following – "Old Tomb Stone: In an old grave yard on the farm of Hugh A. Jones, Esq., is a slate tomb stone [sic], in a good state of preservation, with the following inscription neatly and skillfully executed: In memory of Eleanor Clark, who departed this life January 7th, 1838."

However, in *The Aegis & Intelligencer* on 27 Aug 1886, an article titled "Elenor" (with a poem written by "Osceola" of Claymont, Delaware, on 14 Aug 1886) gave the following information: "On the farm of Mr. Hugh A. Jones, near Conowingo, there is an old grave yard. It is situated on the brow of a high hill and affords a commanding view of the grand scenery along the Susquehanna in northern Harford. The graves are sunken, an occasional stone being placed at the head and foot. There is undoubtedly a history in connection with this consecrated spot. Let the Harford Historical Society unearth and give it to the world. There is only one tombstone in the acres of graves that has an inscription. It is of slate, and in a good state of preservation. The lettering is excellent and as plain as though just completed. It reads 'Elenor Clark, aged 22 years, died 1757.' One hundred and twenty-nine years ago. I append as humble tribute to the memory of Elenor." [A short poem followed].

COALE CEMETERY
("WESTWOOD CEMETERY")

The historic mansion and property *Westwood* is located on Glenville Road, north of Churchville. It is the ancestral home of the Coale family who were related to Samuel Chase, a Signer of the Declaration of Independence. Images of the tombstones were posted on-line at Find-A-Grave by James Turner in 2011. [Information in brackets below was added by Henry C. Peden, Jr. in 2011 and 2015.]

Coale, Eliza Chase, 20 Jun 1788 – 1853 [daughter of Samuel Chase (1741-1811) and his 2nd wife Hannah Kitty Giles, and Eliza Chase was the wife of Skipwith Holland Coale, M.D.]

Coale, Skipwith Holland (Dr.), 1787-1832

Coale, Skipwith Holland Jr. (Dr.), Aug 1822 – 20 Oct 1845

Coale, Thomas Chase, died 11 Jun 1830 [infant son]

Coale, William Freeman [vital information unknown]

Jackson, Eliza Matilda Coale, 6 Apr 1820 – 13 Mar 1904 [wife of Frederick D. Jackson]

Hart, Mary [died 13 Nov ----, buried 15 Nov ----, an African American [according to Leonard Laylon, Cemetery Records Chairman, Historical Society of Harford County, in 2011, citing Holy Trinity Episcopal Church burial records as the source for this burial information]

COEN'S HILL CEMETERY
(see Barnes-Bailey Cemetery)

COLE CEMETERY
This cemetery was once located near Graceford Drive in Aberdeen. Years ago an unidentified researcher copied two tombstones and indicated no other legible stones, noting the cemetery had been partially destroyed by the excavation of gravel. In 2010 development by the Merritt Corporation led to this site becoming an archaeological field site by Gibb Archaeological Consulting and the remains were recovered for probable re-interment in Baker Cemetery. Dr. James Gibb determined that the Cole burial ground contained the remains of 2 adults, 1 infant and 3 children. [Information in brackets below was added by Henry C. Peden, Jr. in 2011.]

Cole, James, 15 Jul 1791 – 4 Jul 1878
[Census records, however, consistently stated he was born in 1794, not 1791. James was a soldier in the War of 1812.]

Cole, Elizabeth Gilbert, 1806-1890, wife of James Cole

COLE – WELLS CEMETERY

This cemetery is located on Roberts Way in Aberdeen. [Information in brackets below added by Henry C. Peden, Jr. in 2015.]

Wells, Mary A., 1 Mar 1809 – 22 Nov 1898
[*The Aegis & Intelligencer* on 25 Nov 1898 reported Mrs. Mary Ann Wells was one of the oldest residents in Harford County when she died at her home near Aberdeen. She had been married twice and her first husband was the late Courtney Cole. She was buried in the family lot on the farm of Mr. O. N. Cole. It was not reported in the newspaper, but other records indicate her second husband was Benjamin N. Wells.]

Footstone: SKC

Footstone: JAC

Footstone: FEC

Cole, William L., died 1863, age 17 years, 11 months and 27 days, son of James C. and Mary A. Cole

Cole, James, died 6 Jul 1851, age 37 years, 3 months and 4 days

R. H. 1806

Rigdon, Charles, died 19 Apr 1815, age 67

COLEMAN GRAVE SITE

John Coleman was buried somewhere on the family farm at Vale. A stone placed inside Christ Episcopal Church, reads: Respectfully dedicated to the memory of John Coleman, Minister of the Protestant Episcopal Church, who departed this life in full assurance tho his earthly house of this

Tabernacle were dissolved, he had a building of God, a house not made with hands, Eternal in the Heavens, 20th January 1816, aged 58 years.

COOLEY CEMETERY

There is no visible sign of this old cemetery, but it is located at "Friendship," the former Cooley farm now owned by a descendant James T. Wollon, Jr. on Craigs Corner Road Eyewitnesses to its location in the early days recalled that the only gravestones were large fieldstones, none in evidence today. Ground penetrating radar clearly found two graves near its southwest corner which is closest to and in clear view of the house, and northeast of the barn, but no other ground disturbances were found in this 104' square lot. Those two ground disturbances were undoubtedly the graves of John Cooley and his wife Sarah Ann Gilbert. [Information above is courtesy of James T. Wollon, Jr. and information in brackets below was added by Henry C. Peden, Jr. in 2015.]

Cooley, John, c1755-1807
[Revolutionary War soldier, 1775-1780]

Cooley, Sarah Ann, c1760-1836

COURTNEY – SILVER GRAVE SITE

Churchville Presbyterian Church's Register of Deaths states "Phebe (Silver) Courtney (Mrs. George)" died 24 Feb 1856 and was buried in the family burying ground. It did not give the name of the family and the location, but stated her name was "obtained from the Diary of James Pannell."

DALLAM CEMETERY
(CRANBERRY CEMETERY)

Identified as Aberdeen Proving Ground Private Cemetery P-1 by the U. S. Government, this cemetery is located on an

16

unidentified road north of the Maryland Gate (Short Lane, Route 715) and west of Bomb Loop. See the binders of *Silent Sentinels of Aberdeen Proving Ground* (1999) at the Historical Society of Harford County in Bel Air, Maryland for tombstone images and further cemetery details. It should also be noted that these tombstones were copied over 50 years ago by an unidentified copyist who then called it Cranberry Cemetery. [Information in brackets below was added by Henry C. Peden, Jr. in 2015.]

Dallam, Edward B., 21 Oct 1822 – 14 Sep 1874

Dallam, Francis J., died 30 Apr 1857, age 70 years, 1 month and 15 days, "Father"

Dallam, Sarah P., died 30 May 1855, age 65 years, 6 months and 19 days, "Mother"

Dallam, Philip R., died 29 Mar 1842, age 53 years, 10 months and 23 days

Carlisle, John W., died 3 Mar 1833, age about 33

Jarrett, Elizabeth Smith, died 24 Oct 1825, age 51 years and 27 days

Dallam, Sarah, died 18 Nov 1797, age 49, wife of J. W.

Dallam, Josias William, died 9 Dec 1820, age 72

Dallam, William M., M.D., 24 Jun 1777 – 6 Apr 1859

Dallam, Frances Smith, died 11 Sep 1830, wife of Dr. William M. Dallam

Spencer, Emily, Miss, died 11 Feb 1849, age – years (stone broken and repaired)

Children of Robert and Elizabeth C. Lockwood
Lockwood, Sallie Wilmer, 5 Sep 1850 – 15 Dec 1860
Lockwood, Edward, 24 Dec 1856 – 3 Dec 1860

Dallam, Francis J., died 14 Jul 1829, age 29 months, son of
F. J. Dallam

Headstone – no markings – slate, broken

Children of Josias W. and Alice Dallam:
Dallam, Frederick Otis, died 2 Jul 1851, age 3 yrs., 9 months
Dallam, Alfred Clifford, died 8 Jul 1851

Dallam, B. Rush, born 9 May 1820, married 18 Oct 1849,
died 7 Nov 1866 [Benjamin Rush Dallam married Jane ----,
but there is no marriage license in Harford Co. for them and
there is no tombstone in this cemetery for wife Jane Dallam]

DAVIDGE CEMETERY
This cemetery is located on the north side of Route 40 on the
former Bata Shoe property at Riverside that was once known
as "Sophia's Dairy" when owned by Col. Aquila Hall who
built the mansion in 1768. The walled cemetery contains just
one monument with four names inscribed, one on each side.
The names were copied by Doris P. Barben in Nov 1987 and
an article and picture were later published in *The Aegis* on 23
Oct 1996 in which Charles Johnston listed the burials, but his
dates were slightly different [as shown in brackets below].

Davidge, W. H. S., consort of Dr. Davidge and youngest
daughter of John Hathor and Agnes Stewart of Physgill
House, Wigtonshire, Scotland, July 19, 1818 [July 12, 1818]

Davidge, John, July 15, 1794 [July 19, 1794]

Davidge, Onner H., August 19, 1791 [Onner Davidge, August 10, 1797]

Davidge, Stewart, July 28, 1800

DAY CEMETERY

In 1926 Capt. Harry W. Spraker published *The Story of Gunpowder Neck* and mentioned two men named Day who were buried on "Rouse Farm – Gun Club." See the binders of *Silent Sentinels of Aberdeen Proving Ground* (1999) at the Historical Society of Harford County in Bel Air, Maryland for tombstone images and further cemetery details. It was also noted by Jon Harlan Livezey that the tombstones were relocated to Private Cemetery P-1-EA (Edgewood Arsenal), but whether or not the bodies were removed is unknown.

Day, John Wesley, died 17 Dec 1832 in his 17th year, son of Goldsmith and Mary S. Day

Day, Goldsmith, died 23 Jan 1840 in his 58th year

DE LA PORTE VAULT

"The Gateway," prepared by The Fallston-Upper Cross Roads Bicentennial Committee circa 1975, stated that *Bon Air* mansion on Laurel Brook Road near Fallston was built by Claudius Francis Frederick de la Porte on a land tract known as *Bond's Forest*. On page 16 they stated "the family cemetery is a low-vaulted stone building beyond the garden with human skeletons in full view." Such is not the case today. These people were known to have been buried there:

Claudius Francis Frederick de la Porte, died 1797

Elizabeth de la Porte, his wife, died 1803

Pierre Francis de la Porte, his brother (no dates given)

DEAVER GRAVE SITE

In 1908 Helen W. Ridgely published *Historic Graves of Maryland and the District of Columbia* (p. 105) and wrote, "On the farm of the late Jeremiah Silver, about a mile east of Harmony Presbyterian Church, is the unmarked grave of Aquila Deaver. According to a well-founded tradition, he bore the illustrious Lafayette on his back from the boat to the Harford shore at the Bald Friar ferry. This occurred in 1781, when the French officer, at the head of the army on his way to Virginia, came to a stand-still owing to the grounding of the boat. He was about to wade ashore, when Deaver presented his brawny shoulders and saved him a wetting." Records, however, indicate Aquila Deaver (1756-1830s) is buried in Row 11 in Angel Hill Cemetery in Havre de Grace.

DORAN CEMETERY

In 2005 an e-mail inquiry was made by Ralph Eshelman, of Lusby, Maryland to Leonard Laylon, Cemetery Records Chairman at the Historical Society of Harford County, with regards to a Doran family cemetery somewhere in Harford County. A later search revealed no information about this cemetery, but records indicate Dorans had lived in the Fourth District. It is possible that the following people, all of whom were Revolutionary War patriots identified by Eshelman, could be buried there, as well as other family members.

Doran, Hugh (1719-1778)

Doran, Edward (1760-1832)

Doran, Patrick (1762-1798)

DORNEY – CUNNINGHAM CEMETERY

In 1926 Capt. Harry W. Spraker published *The Story of Gunpowder Neck* and he mentioned the "Cemetery at Bush

River (Chemical Warfare Depot)." Researchers can now see the binders of *Silent Sentinels of Aberdeen Proving Ground* (1999) at the Historical Society of Harford County in Bel Air, Maryland for tombstone images and further cemetery details. The U. S. Government has named this burial ground located off Bush River Road near 25th Street as Private Cemetery P-1-EA (Edgewood Arsenal).

Dorney, Ida M., died 2 Oct 1858, age 10 months, second daughter of Albert and A. M. Dorney

Dorney, Thomas, died 22 Jan 1844, age 61 years, 2 months and 4 days

Dorney, Emlin W., died 16 Jul 1852, age 10 months and 8 days, son of Albert and A. M. Dorney

Dorney, George W., died 29 Nov 1850, age 2 months, twin child of Jackson and H. J. Dorney

Dorney, Ella L., died 2 Jul 1855, age 2 months and 7 days, daughter of Albert and A. M. Dorney

Dorney, Lizzie J., died 19 Sep 1851, age 1 year, twin child of Jackson and H. J. Dorney

Dorney, Mary, died 22 Mar 1841 in her 51st year, consort of Thomas Dorney

Gibler, Eliza, 7 Feb 1859 – 6 Jul 1862

Hess, Helena L., died 1 Nov 1863, age 2 years, 8 months and 13 days

Cunningham, Levenia Matilda, died 12 Jul 1845, age 9 months and 14 days, daughter of Mortimore and M. E. Cunningham

Dorney, Thomas William, died 13 Jan 1844, age 1 year, 2 months and 21 days

Cunningham, William Henry, died 31 Jan 1851, age 4 years, 8 months, son of Mortimore and M. E. Cunningham

Cunningham, Emely, died 11 Oct 1843, age 5 years and 23 days [Spraker listed her name as Emily Arselia Cunningham]

Cunningham, Albert, d. 10 Nov 1843, age 4 months, 14 days

Headstone – rough – unmarked

These two stones were relocated from "Rouse Farm – Gun Club" on Gunpowder Neck, but whether or not the remains were relocated is unknown:

Day, Goldsmith, died 23 Jan 1840 in his 58th year

Day, John Wesley, died 17 Dec 1832 in his 17th year, son of Goldsmith and Mary S. Day

DORSEY GRAVE SITE

In 1999 Jon Harlan Livezey, Esq., reported to the U. S. Government during the preparation of *Silent Sentinels of Aberdeen Proving Ground* (copy on file at the Historical Society of Harford County in Bel Air, Maryland) that this stone is located on the west side of the road from Maxwell Point Road to "M" Field in the Edgewood Area, and it was exposed during the clearing of the site by CCC forces in August 1936.

Dorsey, Ann, died 8 Jun 1802, age 46

DOVE CEMETERY

Capt. Harry W. Spraker published *The Story of Gunpowder Neck* in 1926 and included a "list of those known to have been buried on Gunpowder Neck." See the binders of *Silent Sentinels of Aberdeen Proving Ground* (1999) at the Historical Society of Harford County in Bel Air, Maryland for tombstone images and further cemetery details. In 1999 the U. S. Government and Jon Harlan Livezey identified this cemetery at Weide Field as the Dove Cemetery. They also cited Charmaine Brankowitz in 1991 who "reports that a cemetery existed at the location on which the present day airport, known as Weide Army Airfield, in the Edgewood Area, was constructed (circa 1941). 'The burial grounds located on the site of the ... runway ... were not removed. However, the tombstones in this area were coated with paraffin and were turned face downward on the graves.' The [exact] location of this cemetery has not been determined." However, the government also stated the "Doves Family" cemetery was reported in 1940 as being in the "Vicinity of C.M.T.C. Camp, Present Location Unknown." [Information in brackets below added by Henry C. Peden, Jr. in 2015.]

Dove, Thomas W., died 5 Jan 1858, age 14

Tucker, Rebecca, died 1839, age 70

Waltham, T. P., died 1810

Waltham, Thomas, died 11 Mar 1845, age 47

Dove, Marmaduke Paul, died 2 Sep 1866, age 44

Dove, William G., died 10 May 1835, age 51
[William Geoghegan Dove, son of Marmaduke Dove and Elizabeth Geoghegan, was a militia lieutenant in the War of

1812. William was born on 3 Mar 1785, married Martha G. Paul (1795-1864) on 18 Jan 1816 in Harford County and died on 10 May 1835.]

Dove, Martha G., died 25 Feb 1864, age 68

Tucker, Elizabeth, died 17 Mar 1816, age 37

Jones, Elizabeth, died 22 Jul 1814, age 62

ENLOWS CEMETERY

The family plot of the James Enlows family was located near Fallston United Methodist Church (formerly known as Friendship Church) in Fallston, but it no longer exists. On 8 Aug 2000 Jeff Fowler contacted Henry C. Peden, Jr. and informed him that the tombstones of James, Prudence and Rebecca Enlows were sold at a public auction in Friendsville in western Maryland and he had acquired them. His intent was to return them to Harford County and then erect them at Fallston United Methodist Church where some other Enlows were buried. Leonard Laylon, Cemetery Records Chairman at the Historical Society of Harford County, offered to assist, but as of this date, over 15 years later, no action had been taken. The names of those buried in this family cemetery were copied by an unidentified copyist "from the Enlow [sic] Family, by E. E. Enlow [sic], Sebastopol, CA, 1948."

Enlows, James, died 17 Jan 1822, age 66

Enlows, Prudence, died 12 Jan 1838, age 81

Enlows, Temperence, died 12 Jul 1853, age 58

Enlows, James Jr., died 13 Mar 1844, age 47

Enlows, Rebecca, died 27 Feb 1867, age 79

FARMER CEMETERY

In 2013 Christopher T. Smithson found the following entry in the notes of local historian George Washington Archer (1824-1907): "In 1712 Gregory Farmer Sr. (planter) bought 50 acres of Margaret's Mount (near ... Westwood) from John Miles (carpenter) of which Farmer sold 10 acres to William Brasier, and in 1751 deeded the rest to his eldest son Samuel who in 1754 sold it to William Cox – except 30 x 30 feet which had been reserved as a graveyard (where his father and mother had been buried) as a burying place for the family. This old graveyard can still be seen though much encroached upon by vandals." Based on this information that was written over 120 years ago it would appear that the following persons, and likely more, were buried in this long lost and forgotten cemetery.

Farmer, Gregory Jr., born 2 Aug 1704, died after 1754

Farmer, Rachel Emson, wife of Gregory Farmer, Jr.

Farmer, Gregory, Sr., father of Gregory Farmer, Jr.

Farmer, Sarah Hughes, wife of Gregory Farmer, Sr.

Farmer, Samuel, born 25 Apr 1721, son of Gregory Farmer, Jr.

Farmer, Elizabeth, wife of Samuel Farmer

GALLUP CEMETERY

The Historical Society of Harford County Archives folder "APG – Spesutia Island #1" contains a brief history of the Gallup family in 1894 by Edward B. Gallup (born 1820) who stated the Gallups moved to Spesutia Island in 1790. "The Gallup family lived on this island many years; many of them died and were buried there. The graveyard is on the upper island farm, and was always called the Gallups' Burying Ground." In an undated *APG News* article titled "Riddle of Spesutia Monument Solved," Miss M. Katherine Taylor explained that when the Spesutia Island Rod & Gun Club acquired the island's Upper Farm of between 500 and 800 acres about 1885 they became aware that the head stones and foot markers of many of the Gallup family graves were consigned to oblivion. "They acted to conserve at least those parts of the scattered and broken markers which today [no date given] are incorporated in what will be henceforth be referred to as the Morgan Manor Marker. No doubt these concerned individuals engaged the services of a mason and instructed him to lay-up the monument in which the bits and pieces are interred. In a sense, then, Aberdeen Proving Ground is the repository of a second Time Capsule, but one which is not slated for opening at any future date. Before this, however, it was noted that the "pile of stones" was in the vicinity of Morgan Manor (Bldg. 1100). There is an indication from Mr. Gallup's history that the following could be buried there. [Information in brackets below was added by Henry C. Peden, Jr. in 2011.]

Gallup, Charles, died 1822, son of Thomas Gallup who died on Spesutia Island

Gallup, Thomas, 25 Aug 1787 – July 1834, son of Charles and Hannah Gallup [*Baltimore American*, 29 Jul 1834, obituary stated he died at his home on Spesutia Island.]

Gallup, Hannah Nicholson, wife of Thomas Gallup

Children of Thomas and Hannah Gallup:

Gallup, Eldridge W., lived to adulthood, possibly buried on Spesutia Island

Gallup, Edward B., lived to adulthood, possibly buried on Spesutia Island

Gallup, Charles T., died young, probably buried on Spesutia Island

Gallup, Thomas Jefferson, died young, probably buried on Spesutia Island

Gallup, Elizabeth, died young, probably buried on Spesutia Island

Gallup, Louisa, died young, probably buried on Spesutia Island

Gallup, Annie Maria, died young, probably buried on Spesutia Island

GHENT CEMETERY
Silent Sentinels of Aberdeen Proving Ground, prepared by the U. S. Government in 1999, stated that Peter and Rachel Ghent (no dates) were reported in 1940 to have been buried in a cemetery in the vicinity of the "Dugout on M Field, Present Location Unknown."

GILBERT CEMETERY
When Joseph L. Hughes copied these tombstones circa the 1950s he stated the cemetery at that time was on land owned by Luther Williamson at Gilbert and Stepney Roads [near Aberdeen on land owned by George Gilbert before 1900]. Its stone walls were capped with slate and measured 30' x 60' approximately. These tombstones were also copied in 1986 by Sally Hesson, Carol Porter and Pat Czerniewski, members of the Baltimore County Genealogical Society. [Information in brackets below added by Henry C. Peden, Jr. in 2011.]

Gilbert, Bennett, 28 Feb 1806 – 16 Dec 1862

Gilbert, Martha S., 16 Nov 1813 – 12 Jan 1902, wife of
Bennett Gilbert [Churchville Presbyterian Church's Register
of Deaths states "Martha Susan (McComas) Gilbert (Mrs.
Bennett)" died on 12 Jan 1901 and was buried in the family
burying ground.]

Gilbert, Elizabeth Ellen, died 29 Mar 1850, age 15 years, 5
months and 2 days

Gilbert, Martha Roberta, died 2 Apr 1850, age 3 months and
12 days

Gilbert, Bennett Gouch [Couch?], died 30 Dec 1818 [1848?],
age 8 months and 9 days

Gilbert, Amos, died 20 Feb 1836, age 62

Gilbert, Sarah, died 14 Aug 1836, age 56
[Churchville Presbyterian Church's Register of Deaths states
"Sarah (Bailey) Gilbert (Mrs. Amos)" died 14 Aug 1836 and
was buried in Gilberts Burying Ground.]

Michael, Naomi, 28 Oct 1785 – 26 Oct 1839, wife of Daniel
Michael

Gilbert, Ellen, 22 May 1816 – 1 Jul 1869, wife of George
Gilbert

Gilbert, George, died 17 Mar 1900, age 85 years, 8 months
and 18 days [Churchville Presbyterian Church's Register of
Deaths states George Alexander Gilbert died on 17 Mar 1900
and was buried in the family burying ground.]

Gilbert, Mary Olevia, 31 Mar 1850 – 12 Oct 1929, daughter
of Bennett Gilbert [Death certificate of M. Olevia Gilbert

stated she was born 31 Mar 1851 and died 12 Oct 1929, age 78 years, 6 months and 11 days – an obvious discrepancy with her tombstone dates.]

Gilbert, George A., 16 Jun 1846 – 25 Aug 1907 [*Havre de Grace Republican*, 31 Aug 1907, stated George Alexander Gilbert, son of Bennett Gilbert and husband of the former Miss Mary Osborn, was buried in the family burying ground on the Gilbert property. Churchville Presbyterian Church's Register of Deaths gives the same burial information. *The Aegis and Intelligencer*, 30 Aug 1907, reported the cemetery was owned by his uncle George Gilbert.]

Gilbert, Mary Silver (no dates), wife of George A. Gilbert [The death certificate of Mary Silver Gilbert, a widow and daughter of Cyrus Osborn and Sarah S. Silver, stated she was born 2 Feb 1845, died 29 Oct 1926 and was buried in Gilbert Family Burying Ground.]

"Harry" – name on small stone; footstone – H. G. McC.

GILBERT CEMETERY

This cemetery no longer exists, but was once located on a horse farm at 740 Gilbert Road known as Twist of Fate Farm when owned by the Holcombs before and after 1986 (see *Harford County Sun*, 13 Jul 1986; the graveyard in the picture is Bennett Gilbert's family burial ground and a different one from this Gilbert cemetery). The Holcomb farm was formerly owned in the late 1700s and early 1800s by Martin Taylor Gilbert's family who were buried there. It is unknown who they all were, but these are some probabilities:

Gilbert, Martin Taylor, 1739-1797
Gilbert, Martha, his wife
Gilbert, Martin Taylor, Jr., 1771-1837
Gilbert, Elizabeth (Treadway), 1780-1838, his wife

GILBERT CEMETERY

Identified as Aberdeen Proving Ground Private Cemetery P-3-EA (Edgewood Arsenal) by the U. S. Government in 1999, this cemetery is located on Ricketts Point Road in the Edgewood Area. They also stated these two graves were reported in 1940 to have been in the "Vicinity of Spring near Gun Club." See the binders of *Silent Sentinels of Aberdeen Proving Ground* (1999) at the Historical Society of Harford County in Bel Air, MD for tombstone images and further cemetery details. [Information in brackets below was added by Henry C. Peden, Jr. in 2015.]

Gilbert, Nelson, died 6 Nov 1899 [African American; 1860 Harford Co. Census indicated he was born c1833]

Gilbert, Hannah, died 9 Jun 1890, wife of Nelson [African American; 1860 Harford Co. Census indicated born c1835]

GOUGH – McCOMAS CEMETERY
(see McComas Grave Sites)

Many years ago an unidentified copyist stated there were "two remaining stones from a small burial ground on the property of Mr. & Mrs. Henry H. Boyer, Moores Mill Road, Bel Air, Maryland, formerly the home of Harry Dorsey Gough." This cemetery no longer exists, although those two markers have survived and were found several years ago in a building on the property known as the Paca's Meadows tract that was planned for development. This latter information was provided circa 2005-2010 by Leonard Laylon, Cemetery Records Chairman, Historical Society of Harford County.

McComas, Preston, died 24 Aug 1837, age 50

McComas, Hannah E., died 11 Jul 1831, age 41

GREENLAND CEMETERY

From an undated record at the Historical Society of Harford County: "This cemetery contained about 40 graves, but only two stones remained when Eldon B. Greenland of Aberdeen, Maryland visited the site a few years ago. Since that time, the remaining stones were bulldozed away to make room for a housing development. This large cemetery, once located on Route 22, a mile north of Carsins Run, no longer exists."

Greenland, Elisha, died 11 Jan 1845, age 55 years, 3 months and 6 days

Thompson, Martha A., 1 Nov 1833 – 17 Apr 1857, wife of William T. Thompson

[Ed. Note: It may interest researchers to know that Ann Greenland, widow of Elisha, died on 31 Jul 1884, age 85, at the residence of her son Richard near Carsins Run and was burial at Calvary Methodist Church (*The Aegis*, 1 Aug 1884). Some other Greenlands are buried in that church cemetery who might have been re-interred from the family cemetery.]

HARDY CEMETERIES

Silent Sentinels of Aberdeen Proving Ground, prepared by the U. S. Government in 1999, stated that it was reported in 1940 that there was a Hardy family cemetery in the vicinity of Lauderick's Creek and another one in the vicinity of the Old Gravel Pit, but no names were given. They also stated that the present locations of these cemeteries are not known.

HAYS – JARRETT CEMETERY
(see Jarrett Grave Site)

This cemetery was once located on the old Archer Hays farm that is now the campus of Harford Community College. Its exact location is undetermined. The inscriptions were copied by local historian George W. Archer in August 1889. The tombstones, but not the remains, were moved to Churchville Presbyterian Church later (date not known). [Information in brackets below was added by George W. Archer in 1889.]

Hays, Archer, died July 1827, age 71

Hays, Hanna[h], died 26 Mar 1847, in her 91st year, wife of Archer Hays

Hays, William S., died 1949, age 50, son of Archer and Hannah Hays

Jarrett, Abraham, died 19 Jul 1832, age 47

Jarrett, Elizabeth S., died 19 Aug 1860, age 74, wife of Abraham Jarrett [daughter of Archer and Hannah Hays]

Jarrett, Elizabeth, died 3 Mar 1850, age 19 years and 6 months daughter [daughter of Abraham and Elizabeth]

Jarrett, John T., died 22 Jun 1829, age 11 months, son [of Abraham]

Smith, William, died 4 Jun 1837, age 74 [Mrs. Hays' brother]

[David Hopkins (1770-1822), an Englishman, was a master mason who built the Hays-Heighe House in 1808 and the D. H. Spring House in 1816. He lived on the Hays property, now part of Harford Community College, and may have been buried in their cemetery, but there is no grave marker.]

HEAPS CEMETERY

This cemetery is on the south side of Neal Road, about ½ mile west of Onion Road, in the northern part of the county. An unidentified copyist circa the 1960s stated the cemetery "is enclosed in a wire fence with slate fence posts and is overgrown. There appears to be seven (7) rows of graves, most of which are marked with field stone. Listed below are the graves that could be identified." Some additional graves were identified in a Maryland Historical Trust Inventory taken circa 1970s and later by Henry C. Peden, Jr. and Jack L. Shagena, Jr. in 2010. The property was owned by John Heaps in 1880 (*The Aegis*, 8 Oct 1880) and later owned by Dale W. Heaps by the 1970s. MHT (HA-914) called it the Heaps-Wright Family Graveyard. [Information in brackets below was added by Henry C. Peden, Jr. in 2011]

Heaps, John, died 1852, age 92

Heaps, Charity, 7 Mar 1772 – 10 Apr 1855 [neé Brindley; MHT mistakenly stated 1782-1855]

Heaps, Mary, died 7 Jun 1869, age 77 years, 2 months and 5 days, daughter of John and Charity Heaps; copyist in 1960s gave year of death as 1889 and MHT stated 1788-1855, but the correct dates would actually be 2 Apr 1792 – 7 Jun 1869]

Houston, John, 10 Jan 1788 – 12 Mar 1852

Brindley, Nathaniel [L.], died 26 Sep 1880, age 86 years, 7 months and 25 days [MHT incorrectly stated 1795-1830; *The Aegis and Intelligencer*, 8 Oct 1880, stated Nathaniel L. Brindley died near Five Forks in upper Harford County on Sunday night, 26 Sep 1880, in his 87th year, and was buried in the private burying ground on Mr. John Heaps' farm.]

Brindley, Sarah, died 29 Jan 1879, age 85 years, 1 month and 5 days [neé Heaps; MHT mistakenly stated 1794-1877]

Miller, William H., 1874 – [sic]

Miller, Alice C., 1875-1932 [neé Heaps]

Taylor, Nancy, 16 Feb 1798 – 18 Oct 1879 [Ann Taylor, age 60 in 1860 census; Nancy Taylor, age 72 in 1870 census)

Taylor, Corbin, 1830-1892(?) [son of Nancy Taylor; MHT gave dates as 1850-1892]

Bose, John H., 10 Feb 1843 – 17 Jul 1860, son of William and Charity Bose [MHT gave the dates as 1848-1860; Bose was spelled Bosh in the 1877/1879 will of Nancy Taylor.]

Bose, Harvey A., 1855-1860, son of William and Charity Bose [complete dates unknown; Bose was spelled Bosh in the 1877/1879 will of grandmother Nancy Taylor.]

Bose, Corbin T., died 1848, son of William and Charity Bose [complete dates unknown; Bose was spelled Bosh in the 1877/1879 will of grandmother Nancy Taylor.]

Taylor, Corbin, died 19 Feb 1837, age 42 years, 8 months and 9 days [This would make his birth date 1 Jun 1794, but a church record indicates born 27 Aug 1791; his tombstone was laid flat and completely covered in a layer of dirt and leaves; Jack Shagena literally stumbled across it in 2011; Corbin Taylor was a militia private during the War of 1812.]

HILL CEMETERY

On 10 Dec 1886 *The Aegis and Intelligencer* reported in the column "Bush River Neck Affairs" that "Mrs. Martha Hill, widow of John Fletcher Hill, died of typhoid pneumonia on Tuesday of last week, at the house of Ben Mahomet, where she was employed as a housekeeper. She was buried in the family burying ground, near Mr. Charles B. Gilbert's, on Wednesday … G. Osborn & Sons, undertakers." [Ed. Note: John Fletcher Hill married Martha N. Ford in February 1859 in Harford County and both were born circa 1835.]

HILL – JOHNSON CEMETERY

In the 1950s Joseph L. Hughes wrote that this cemetery "located between Evans Corner and Havre de Grace on left side of road to Havre de Grace in edge of wood … size about 100' x 336' [contained] hundred or more graves not marked, others marked with field stones. Sunken in earth in all directions, indicating graves, very large burial ground, thought to be colored, a few stones follow." Jon Harlan Livezey also copied the markers in the 1960s. It has also been noted that this cemetery is about one-half mile east of the intersection of Chapel Road with Earlton Road and this is an African American cemetery. [Information in brackets was added below by Henry C. Peden, Jr. in 2015.]

Hill, Jerome, died 23 Aug 1870, age 18 years and 3 days, son of Mary Ann Hill

Hill, Aquila, 18 Dec 1839 – 17 Jan 1909, son of James and Milcah Hill [Death certificate of Aquila Hill stated his parents were James Hill and Milcah Aikens.]

Hill, James, died 13 Sep 1860 in 62nd year, My Father

Hill, Louis, Co. H, 28 U. S. Cav. (no dates) [There was a Lewis H. Hill who served as a corporal in Co. G, 30th MD Regiment Infantry, U.S.C.T., 28 May 1864 – 10 Dec 1865.]

Johnson, Mary Ann, died 14 Jan 1871 in 62nd year [neé Hill], wife of George A. Johnson

Brown, Mary Ann, died 23 Jan 1871, age 6 months and 19 days, granddaughter of Mary Johnson

Curtis, Josephine, 31 Jan 1847 – 10 Nov 1866, wife of Freeborn Curtis

HOWARD GRAVE SITE

The death certificate of Luther Howard, of Havre de Grace, stated he had died on 4 Dec 1942, age 65, and was buried in "Osborne's Cemetery." Since there is more than one Osborn or Osborne Cemetery, and Luther Howard has no tombstone, it is not yet determined which cemetery he rests in.

HOWLETT GRAVE SITE

An unidentified researcher stated that a "Howlett Cemetery" was near Mt. Erin Catholic Cemetery in Havre de Grace and the tombstones were in bad shape with only one that could be read, namely John R. Howlett. This undated note implied that this was a family cemetery, but it may be referring to the old Cedar Hill Cemetery. The marker for John R. Howlett states he died 7 Feb 1848, age 25 years and 9 months. There are only a few other stones and it is uncertain whether or not Howlett was buried there initially or re-interred from a family cemetery; therefore, it was decided to mention this cemetery just in case.

INDIAN GRAVE SITE

"Tribes of Indians had their settlements at or near the Rocks of Deer Creek ... a village of Susquehannocks was, in 1680, located near what was formerly the La Grange Iron Works ... This spot is near the present bridge ... [Rocks Road at St. Clair Bridge Road] ... Five miles above, near the Stansbury Mill at Red Bridge, was the tribe known as Mingoes and two and one-half miles southeast of Rocks was another Indian village. Legend tells the story of one, Mingo by name, who returned to dwell among the whites. Married to Watumpka, who was captured from the Wicomocoes, he remained with her until her death and burial by the creek among the trees. Residents today [1967] point out the marking stones of an Indian grave, not far from the king and queen seat, which may be the resting place of Mingo, who desired to live and die among the hills he knew so well." (Source: *Our Harford Heritage*, by C. Milton Wright (1967), p. 94)

INDIAN GRAVE SITE

John Love's Field Book dates to the early 1700s and it was abstracted by Henry Wilson Archer in 1894. On page 135 is the survey of a 100-acre tract called *Jericho* for Thomas Stansbury in 1745. It states, in part, "Beginning at two white oaks in the fork of the two small draughts of Indian Grave Run which descends into Gunpowder River ..." Obviously, to get such a name, the stream must have been the site of an Indian grave whose identify we will most likely never know.

JARRETT GRAVE SITE
(see Hays-Jarrett Cemetery)

Churchville Presbyterian Church's Register of Deaths states Elizabeth Jarrett, daughter of Abraham Jarrett and Elizabeth Hays, died 3 Mar 1850 and was buried on the "Joseph Jacobs farm, later to Churchville." [Ed. Note: The 1858 Jennings & Herrick Map of Harford County shows the J. Jacobs property on the north side of Churchville Road where the Harford Community College is today. Elizabeth Jarrett, died 3 Mar 1850, age 19 years, 6 months, now rests in the Churchville Presbyterian Church Cemetery beside her parents. There are no markers in that cemetery for Joseph Jacobs so it appears that he and possibly other Jacobs family members are buried on the old farm, now the college campus, without markers.]

JEFFERS CEMETERY

Benjamin Jeffers owned 200 acres called "Maxwell's Conclusion" on lower Gunpowder Neck, at Maxwell Point, about eight miles from Magnolia. He was originally from the Eastern Shore of Maryland and was age 49 in the 1850 Harford County census. The family cemetery is now underwater, the land having been reclaimed by the bay.

Some have called it Maxwell Point Cemetery. The first wife of Benjamin, Henrietta Roach or Rouch, whom he married in 1826, is buried here. His second wife Sarah Ann Stapleford (1825-1900), whom he married in 1855, and some other Jeffers, are buried at Cokesbury United Methodist Church in Abingdon. Benjamin's obituary appeared in the *Baltimore Sun* on 19 May 1865. The only known burials in Jeffers Cemetery are as follows.

Jeffers, Benjamin, c1801 – 4 May 1865

Jeffers, Laura, 1861-1865, daughter of Benjamin Jeffers

Jeffers, Henrietta, c1804-c1854, wife of Benjamin Jeffers

JERICHO GRAVEYARD
(Lee Grave Sites)

An unidentified copyist had stated this cemetery was on the Jericho farm on Tobacco Run [i.e., on the south side of Cool Spring Road]. *A Short Biography of Those Whose Portraits Adorn the Walls of the Court House, Bel Air, Maryland*, by Frederick Lee Cobourn (1942), p. 33, states, in part, Parker Hall Lee "died May 6, 1829, and was buried at Jericho [farm situated between Deer Creek and Thomas Run] in the private graveyard on that property, enclosed by a large stone wall." David Warnick took pictures of the marker and the house several years ago. Maryland Historical Trust File HA-909, prepared about forty years ago, called it the Jericho family graveyard and stated "stone wall surrounds family graveyard of about 8 to 14 graves on a knoll south of the manor house Jericho." They also referred to it as "Lee and Archer family graveyard." When the two remaining markers were copied many years ago the graveyard was then on the property of Mr. & Mrs. James Barrow in the Thomas Run Valley, about 250 yards northeast of the old home which was still standing,

38

but then in ruins. [The information in brackets above and below was added by Henry C. Peden, Jr. in 2015 and in 2016 with assistance from researcher Christopher T. Smithson.]

Lee, Parker Hall, 1759-1829
[Parker Hall Lee served as a lieutenant in the Revolutionary War and died 6 Jun 1829.]

Lee, Elizabeth Dallam, 1757-1808, his [first] wife
[Parker Hall Lee's second wife Mary (1776-1860) is buried at Rock Spring Church.]

JOHNSON CEMETERY

"The Gateway," prepared by The Fallston-Upper Cross Roads Bicentennial Committee circa 1975-1976, stated that the Harrison place was the second farm north of Upper Crossroads on the west side of Jarrettsville – Baldwin Mill Road. "In 1822 John B. Johnson married Elizabeth Hawkins. In the family burying ground near the house is a gravestone for John B. Johnson dated 1847." [Information in brackets below was added by Henry C. Peden, Jr. in 2015]

Johnson, Mary E., died 27 Apr 1874 in her 50th year

Withers, Mrs. Caroline R. (H.?), our dear aunt, died 20 Dec 1894 in her 69th year

Johnson, John B., died 20 Sep 1847, age 48 [wife Elizabeth probably buried here]

JONES CEMETERY

Amos Jones was a private in the Harford County militia during the Revolutionary War. His grave site was found in 1977 after a diligent search by Joseph Carroll Hopkins, who was a descendant. The Harford Town Chapter, DAR, along with the Col. Aquila Hall Chapter, SAR, restored the Jones

Cemetery and in a ceremony conducted on 21 Sep 1981 they placed a DAR marker beside the tombstone of Amos Jones. References to the cemetery are found in Harford County land records in 1842 and 1965. Its location in 1977 was described as being "in Fallston, 3rd District, near Laurel Brook Drive, to the rear of the property now owned by Milton W. Martin. To reach the graveyard from Fallston, enter Rochelle Drive and go to the end of the drive at the edge of the woods. This property is part of 'Bond's Forest and Addition.' The graveyard is part of 'Addition' and consists of one quarter of an acre as specified in a deed dated April 6, 1842, Harford County Land Record HD 26, folio 305 ..." This is a land conveyance from Hugh Jones et al. to Benjamin P. Moore. [Information in brackets below added by Henry C. Peden, Jr. in 2015.]

Jones, Amos, died 12 Sep 1827, age 75 [born 23 Jul 1754]

Jones, Ann, died 2 Jun 1850, age 95, consort of Amos Jones [neé Lewin]

Jones, Amos, 29 Oct 1813 – 27 Sep 1823

Adkinson [sic], Ann, 23 Aug 1796 – 3 Feb 1828

Jones, Daniel, died 14 Apr 1848, age 64

Atkinson [sic], Ann, died 2 Feb 1823, age 28, consort of David Atkinson [sic] and daughter of Amos and Ann Jones

Jones, Rebekah 12 Sep 1787-16 Apr 1825 [neé Scarborough; wife of Daniel Jones]]

Jones, Sarah Ann, 17 Apr 1816 – 20 Oct 1823 [daughter of Daniel and Rebekah Jones]

Jones, Emeline, 14 Jan 18187 – 20 Oct 1823 [daughter of Daniel and Rebekah Jones]

Thompson, Mary, died 2 Aug 1833, age 32, consort of William Thompson and daughter of Amos and Ann Jones

JONES – JARRETT CEMETERY

This family burying ground no longer exists. It was located on "Stockdale" farm south of the intersection of Emmorton Road (Route 924) and Patterson Mill Road. Formerly the property of the late Thomas Brookes, and before him the Farnandis, Taylor and Jones families, the burying ground was likely located somewhere between what is now the site of the Lorien of Bel Air Rehabilitation Center and the Patterson Mill Fire Station. There are no grave markers to be found, but some people that were known to have been buried here were as follows. [Information researched by Henry C. Peden, Jr. and Christopher T. Smithson in 2011.]

Jarrett, Abram Lingan, 5 Sep 1808 – 18 Feb 1894 [obituary in *The Aegis & Intelligencer*, 23 Feb 1894, reported "the interment being by the side of his wife, in the family burying ground on a portion of the Farnandis farm, formerly belonging to his wife's family." From other sources it was learned that Jarrett was a captain and very prominent man, having served as Clerk of the County Court for many years.]

Jarrett, Mary Ann Elizabeth, c1809 – 2 Jun 1888 [daughter of Stephen Jones; her obituary in *The Aegis & Intelligencer*, 8 Jun 1888, stated she died in her 79th year, "the interment being in the burial ground of her ancestors, on the Taylor farm, now comprising part of the farm of Hon. Henry D. Farnandis]

Jones, Sallie Cassandra (Miss), 1815 – 30 Jan 1905 [obituary in the *Bel Air Times*, 3 Feb 1905, stated she died in her 90th year and "was born upon the Stockdale farm, now known as the Farnandis place, near Bel Air … a sister-in-law of the late Captain A. Lingan Jarrett … the interment being made in the family burying ground at Stockdale." Death certificate of Sallie Cassandra Jones stated she was age 89 and her parents were Stephen Jones and Mary Taylor.]

Jones, Stephen, father of Mary Ann Elizabeth Jarrett, is probably buried here also.

LAPIDUM GRAVE SITE

The following article appeared in the *Havre de Grace Republican* on 8 Aug 1873: "*Skeletons Discovered.* – Dr. W. W. Virdin, whilst making an excavation in the side of a bank near Lapidum, opposite Port Deposit, for the purpose of erecting a coal shed and yard, discovered the skeletons of two bodies, one measuring over seven feet, and strange to say a large brass key was found lying across his breast bone; the wood work of the coffin all decayed. – *Cecil Democrat.*"

LEE GRAVE SITES
(see Jericho Graveyard)

LEE GRAVE SITE

The following graves are located in the side of the front yard on the property of Mrs. Audrey Concini at 1114 N. Tollgate Road. On a visit in 2007 Henry C. Peden, Jr. and Jack L. Shagena, Jr. were told the grave markers had been moved a few feet to the south to allow for the construction of a shed, but the bodies remained in their original graves.

Lee, David, 13 Sep 1778 – 4 Dec 1851
Lee, Deborah, 11 Feb 1776 – 15 Apr 1859

LEGOE CEMETERY

Identified as Aberdeen Proving Ground Private Cemetery P-2-EA (Edgewood Arsenal) by the U. S. Government, this cemetery is located off Ricketts Point Road on 57th Street atop a slope close to Bush River. See the binders of *Silent Sentinels of Aberdeen Proving Ground* (1999) at the Historical Society of Harford County in Bel Air, Maryland for tombstone images and further cemetery details. In 1962 an unidentified copyist stated the approximately 30' x 30' cemetery was in back of Bldg. 330 and it had many sunken places in it. [Information in brackets below added by Henry C. Peden, Jr. in 2015.]

Legoe, Ellen B. [R.?], died 30 Jul 1859, age 33, wife of Capt. S. Legoe [Salathiel Legoe was a mariner, not a military captain; he married Ellen Roberts in 1830, thus the initial B that was copied from her marker might actually be an R; Salathiel died in 1864 and is probably buried here as well.]

Two other headstones – rough – unmarked

LEWIS FAMILY VAULT
In 1924 J. Frank Mitchell had charge of the Bloomsbury estate near Havre de Grace. *The Aegis* reported on 11 Jan 1924 that the Lewis family vault on Upper Bloomsbury farm was constructed in 1852 of heavy granite and iron and contained tiers for nine bodies. It was reportedly so badly damaged by vandals that it was no longer waterproof. The two bodies (names not given) that had been interred there were then removed to Philadelphia.

LITTLE PINES CEMETERY
Maryland Historical Trust Inventory File HA-601 contains limited information about an old, possibly 19th century, graveyard at Little Pines Farm in Darlington. Around 1970 Harold E. Harvey owned the property and informed MHT that "Mr. Mason [Samuel Mason was a local historian and the former owner of the property] had learned from neighbors and found traces of human bones at this site, so he left this ground undisturbed and planted a dwarf pine here to

mark the burial ground of unknown family members or slaves or perhaps Indians." There are no signs of this cemetery today. [Information in brackets above was added by Henry C. Peden, Jr. in 2015.]

McCOMAS GRAVE SITES
(see Gough-McComas Cemetery)

Maryland Historical Trust File HA-933 was prepared in the 1970s and pertains to the house and property at Southampton Farm located at 1112 Moores Mills Road that was once owned by Harry Dorsey Gough (1792-1867), a prominent Harford County citizen and War of 1812 veteran. The file states, in part, "A small grave plot was found north west of the house, several years ago. This had two tombstones – both in surprizingly [sic] good shape. One was for 'Hannah W. [sic], wife of Preston McComas, who died July 11, 1831 …' and the other for Preston McComas who died August 24, 1837." [Ed. Note: Preston McComas (1787-1837), son of Alexander McComas, married Hannah Eliza Gough (1790-1831) who was the daughter of Harry Dorsey Gough and he (Harry) is buried at Christ Episcopal Church Cemetery.]

McFADON GRAVE SITE

A resurvey of *Mary's Lot* in 1783 mentioned in the metes and bounds "a place called McFadon's grave." In 1871 Henry Wilson Archer copied this survey and indicated "this stone lies S.11 3/4° E., 4 84/100 ps. [perches] from a stone at the end of the '26th line' of Green Spring Forest." He also cited "a stone in a valley [in Jeremiah P. Silver's field]" and later mentioned "a stone marked 'GUM' by a branch [near Harmony Church]."

MICHAEL CEMETERY

This cemetery is located about a half mile to the east of Old Post Road (Route 7) between Swan Creek and Monroe

Avenue and is situated in a trailer park. It is on a tract of land originally owned by Baltsher Michael who had purchased it circa 1740 and in 1959, when the markers were copied it was known as the Calvin Michael farm. {Information in braces below by Joseph Lee Hughes who stated the cemetery was restored with concrete posts and pipe in 1959.} [Information in brackets below was added by Henry C. Peden, Jr., 2015.]

Michael, Baltsher, died 14 Feb 1795, a native of Germany [probably born 21 Dec 1729. His grave was marked with a soldier's marker by the Gov. William Paca Chapter, DAR, Michael Baltsher served in the French & Indian War and in the Revolutionary War.]

Michael, Ann, neé Obsorn, died 30 Aug 1834 [born 1748]

Michael Daniel, died 26 Jul 1853 in his 79th year [born 2 Feb 1774] [He was a militia private during the War of 1812.]

Unmarked stone beside Daniel Michael {This is either his first wife Martha Horner, born 2 Feb 1783 and died 26 Sep 1818, or his second wife Nancy Greenfield, but no dates.}

Michael, Jacob (colonel), died 20 Jan 1853, age 82 years and 5 months [He was a captain in the 42nd Militia Regiment in the War of 1812.]

Michael, Mary, consort of Capt. Jacob Michael, died 29 Mar 1803 in her 31st year

Michael, Effa Courtney, died 25 Apr 1834 in her 28th year {1st wife of Henry E. Michael}

MILLER CEMETERY

This small cemetery lies in ruins in a field, slated for development, about 250 yards north of the 4100 block of Webster-Lapidum Road. Mary Moses stated she grew up in this area and thought it was the Simmons family graveyard, but no one by that name was found when Henry C. Peden, Jr. and Jack L. Shagena, Jr. visited the site on 15 May 2015.

Miller, Thomas, 1 Jun 1810 – 15 Aug 1889 [large stone lying flat, but very legible]

Miller(?), Abram L. J., 11 Sep 1841(?) – 11 Nov 11 1854(?), son of ---- and ---- Miller(?) [small tombstone very illegible and quite weathered]

Footstone: G. M.

MITCHELL – OSBORN CEMETERY

When copied on 27 Nov 1959 this cemetery was noted as being located on Chapel Road on the Story farm and Joseph Lee Hughes called it the Kent Mitchell Burying Ground. He also noted that it was "between Story farm & Reese Gilbert & Gatto, on Story farm." Hughes indicated the cemetery was approximately 150' long and 50' wide and there were dozens of gray field stones set up in rows without any markings on them. [Information in brackets below was added by Henry C. Peden, Jr. in 2016.]

Thompson, Ann, died 6 Feb 1815, age 41, wife of Joshua

Mitchell, Kent, died 9 Mar 1850, age 61

Osborn, Bennett, 10 May 1810 – 23 Sep 1867

Field stone: P. E., April 1825

Field stone: C. H. (no date)

Mitchell, Ann Martha, died 25 Sep 1824, age 24, wife of John Mitchell, Sr.

Mitchell, Parker, 8 Oct 1822 – 18 Oct 1822, son of Ann M. and John Mitchell, Sr.

Field stone: E. T. 1797

Osborn, Elizabeth, 14 Sep 1803 – 20 Aug 1868

Osborn, Martha, died 10 Jun 1853, age 70 years, 2 months and 8 days, wife of Aquilla Osborn

Osborn, Aquilla, died 11 Nov 1848, age 75 years, 10 months and 11 days

Osborn, Martha C., died 1 Nov 1839, age 15 years, 6 months and 23 days, daughter of Martha and Aquilla Osborn

Osborn, Susanna, died 11 Oct 1831, age 13 years, 8 months and 17 days, daughter of Martha and Aquilla Osborn

Field stone: J. A. M. (no date)

[In 1953 Joseph Lee Hughes stated the following children of Evan Thomas Hughes (1837-1921) and wife Sarah Frances Gorrell (1848-1908) were buried in the Kent Mitchell grave yard, which he noted in his book *The Hughes Genealogy, 1636-1953*, p. 113. Evan and Sarah Frances Hughes are not buried here, but they are interred in Rock Run Cemetery.]

Hughes, Melissa Lorenda, eldest child, died 1867, infant

Hughes, Hannah Elizabeth, second child, died 1868, infant

Hughes, May, fifth child, died 1874, infant

Hughes, Everett Gilbert, seventh child, died 1877, infant

Hughes, William Ward "Willie," fourth child, 27 Feb 1872 – 8 Oct 1884

Hughes, Charles E., eighth child, 18 Jan 1879 – 7 Oct 1884

Hughes, Margaret A. "Maggie," ninth child, 3 Feb 1875 – 7 Oct 1884
[*The Aegis and Intelligencer* reported on 31 Oct 1884 that the last three Hughes children named above, Willie, Charles and Maggie, all died of diphtheria.]

MORGAN CEMETERY
Silent Sentinels of Aberdeen Proving Ground, prepared by the U. S. Government in 1999, stated that it was reported in 1940 that the Morgan family cemetery (no names given) was located in the "Field East of Fort Hoyle Commissary, Present Location Unknown."

NORRIS CEMETERY
The Harford Democrat, 24 Jan 1890, reported "Robert W. Norris, of Baltimore, formerly of Harford, had the remains of his father, mother and brother removed from the old Norris property, near Wilna, now occupied by Wm. C. Bavington, to Union Chapel." [There are tombstones in Union Chapel Cemetery on Old Joppa Road for several Norrises, including Robert Wesley Norris (1822-1903) and his wife Catherine Ann Norris (1824-1872, neé Young). Robert W. Norris was the son of Rhesa Norris and Susannah Dutton (1809-1835).]

OAKINGTON GRAVE SITE
In 1936 L. Fickenscher, of Oakington Farms, wrote that this is "one of the most beautiful estates of the upper bay region of Maryland, located in Harford County, just off U. S. Highway 50 between Havre de Grace and Aberdeen. The original tract of land of 800 acres was surveyed in 1659 for Col. Nathaniel Utie …

[who] conveyed 300 acres to Ruthen Garrett [1672]. Thomas Browne, according to the original rent rolls, became the possessor of the remaining 500 acres. His grave is near the mansion house." In 1935 Oakington was purchased by U. S. Senator Millard E. Tydings.

OSBORN CEMETERY

On 29 Mar 1892 George W. Archer copied this cemetery, noting "The Osborn Graveyard on the farm of Chas. B. Osborn upon which Cyrus Osborn formerly resided who followed his father Amos Osborn in ownership, *Blenheim* [sketch of graveyard and list of graves]. The foregoing list includes all the graves with marks (sic). There are a great many more having common stones." A later unidentified copyist noted that the cemetery is on Robin Hood Road at the corner of New Robin Hood Road. [Information in brackets below was added by Henry C. Peden, Jr. in 2015.]

Osborn, Harriet, 24 Dec 1795 – 19 Oct 1833

Osborn, John, born 18 May 1796(?) – stone broken

Osborn, Amos, died 7 Jul 1841 in his 75th year

1806 E + O (soapstone)
Elizabeth Osborn died in 1806, age 30

Mitchell, Thomas, died 5 Nov 1814 in his 42nd year
[Thomas served in the War of 1812.]

Barnes, Eleanor, died 14 Apr 1849 in her 72nd year

OSBORN(E) CEMETERY

Identified as Aberdeen Proving Ground Private Cemetery P-5 by the U. S. Government, this cemetery is located on the Abbey Point Road near Old Baltimore Road and Redman Cove. Also see the binders of *Silent Sentinels of Aberdeen Proving Ground* (1999) at the Historical Society of Harford County in Bel Air, MD for tombstone images and further cemetery details. [Information in brackets below added by Henry C. Peden, Jr. in 2015.]

Reed, C. C. Elizabeth J., died 2 Nov 1858, age 15 years, 7 months and 24 days [Unidentified copyist in 1958 indicated her first name could not be read, did not list her age and also misspelled her father's name as Morris.]

Ruff, Elizabeth, died 6 Mar 1826 in her 38th year, consort of H. P. Ruff [Unidentified copyist in 1958 listed her name as Elizabeth U. Ruff.]

Denny, Lucy, died 21 Aug 1856 in her 67th year, wife of Thomas Denny

Osborn, Benjamin, died 4 Aug 1850 in his 33rd year

Greenlee, Sarah A. R., died 13 Nov 1859 in her 35th year, wife of John Greenlee

Greenlee, John, 17 Apr 1812 – 2 Feb 1871

Michael, John Osborn, 18 May 1811 – 12 Oct 1880, son of Col. Jacob and Susannah

Michael, Susannah, died 26 Sep 1826 in her 51st year, consort of Col. Jacob Michael

Cole, Martha, died 8 Jan 1861 in her 72nd year, our mother

Reasin, William Henry, died 23 Jun 1852, age 9 months and 3 weeks, only son of William H. and Hannah E. Reasin [No marker was found in 1999]

Greenlee, Margaret, 19 Apr 1819 – 13 Apr 1832

[No marker was found in 1999, but a 1958 transcription indicated she was a wife of John Greenlee]

Cole, Catherine, died 2 Nov 1840, age 65
[No marker was found in 1999 when Jon Harlan Livezey indicated government records gave her age as 66]

Cole, James, died 17 Nov 1831 [1851?], age 59
[No marker found in 1999 when Jon Harlan Livezey indicated government records gave his year of death as 1851]

Greenlee, John Henry, died 30 Apr 1960, age 6 months, son of John & S. A. R. Greenlee

Chesney, Daniel C., died 4 Feb 1848, age 9 months [No marker was found in 1999]

Lester, Martha R., 30 Jan 1817 – 5 Mar 1870 [No marker was found in 1999]

Ruff, Octavian H., died 25 Aug 1850 in his 52nd year
[No marker was found in 1999, but a 1958 transcription misspelled his name Actavian and did not give his age]

OWENS CEMETERY
Silent Sentinels of Aberdeen Proving Ground, prepared by the U. S. Government in 1999, stated that it was reported in 1940 that the Owens family cemetery (no names given) was located on "Bell Farm, Present Location Unknown."

PARKER CEMETERY
This cemetery is located on the north side of Wilkinson Road just east of Craigs Corner. One copyist in 1955 stated the property was then owned by Mrs. Wakefield. In 1979 Mary Bristow stated it was located slightly down hill towards the

Susquehanna River in front of the present workshop of the Susquehanna State Park. Some of the markers are difficult to read and Christopher T. Smithson recopied several of them in July 2010. [His corrected information and remarks by Henry C. Peden, Jr. are shown below in brackets.]

Stephenson, Ann P., 11 Mar 1810 – 9 Feb 1892 [*The Aegis & Intelligencer*, 19 Feb 1892, stated Ann P. Stephenson, aged 82, sister of the late Col. William H. Stephenson, near Garland, died on 9 Feb 1892 at the residence of her nephew William Stephenson and she was interred in the old family burying ground in the neighborhood on 12 Feb 1892.]

Hopkins, Mrs. Hannah P. (and Babe), d. 13 Apr 1843, age 30

Stephenson, Susannah, died 17 [actually 19], 1858, age 16

Stephenson, Cassandra, 25 Jun 1803 – 28 Mar 1859

Parker, Nancy G., died 1891, age 83

Jacobs, Hetty S., died 10 Nov 1809 [incorrect date], age 52 [Hetty S. Parker married Charles Watters Jacobs circa 2 May 1833 and her obituary stated she died 11 Nov 1861.]

Parker, Joseph Coudon, 4 Jan 1804 – 16 Sep 1892

Parker, Sarah H., 1 Oct 1809 – 22 Mar 1893 [Sarah H. Stephenson married Joseph Coudon circa 3 Jun 1835. An unidentified tombstone copyist mistakenly listed her name as Hannah H. Parker. Mary Bristow in 1979 and Smithson in 2010 copied it as Sarah.]

Parker, Lucy, 14 Feb 1847 – 1 Jan 1900

Parker, Edward, died 1907, age 91

Parker, Margery, died 4 Nov 1843, age 60, our mother and wife of Joseph Parker [Mary Bristow copied the marker in 1979 as "Marjorie Parker, died 1? Nov 1843, 70 years."]

Parker, Joseph, died 11 Jun 1810 [sic], age 76, "our father" [Joseph Parker actually died in 1840]

Stephenson, William, died 6 Sep 1899 [sic] in his 71st year [actually died 6 Dec 1839 in his 74th year, as copied by Mary Bristow in 1979], a local minister of the Methodist Church

Stephenson, Hetty, died 3 Aug 1854 in her 54th year [actually in her 83rd year], widow of Rev. William Stephenson [Mary Bristow in 1979 copied her death as 3 Aug 1856, age 83.]

Stephenson, Mary A., Mistress [Mrs.], sister, died 3 Oct 1811[?] in her 12th [?] year

Parker, Henry, died 14 Feb 1860 in his 8th year, son of Joseph and Sarah Parker

Parker, Norman, died 23 Apr 1851, age 11 months and 23 days, son of Joseph and Sarah Parker

Parker, Carrie, age 9 years and 2 months

Stephenson, Eliza, died 30 Oct 1839, age 30 or 36 [Smithson stated "stone destroyed"]

Cooley, Mary, Mistress [Mrs.], died 28 Sep 1839 in her 36th year [actually 56th year]

Stephenson, James, died 9 Apr 1838 [actually 1858], age 70 years, 7 months, 20 days

Stephenson, Priscilla, 20 Sep 1777 – 17 Feb 1861 (1866?) in her 84th year

[Mary Bristow in 1979 copied this name as Priscilla Hopkins and her year of death as 1861. Smithson in 2010 copied her name as Priscilla Stephenson and stated the year could be 1861 or 1866.]

D. L. 1802

Dicory, a native of Great Britain, died September 11, 1809, aged 50 years, this man, seaman on British vessel, died with yellow fever and buried at night.

Stephenson, Mary, died April 1871 in his 72nd (77th?) year, daughter of George and Sarah Stephenson [Smithson stated this information was on a new stone.]

Wakefield, Arthur Frank, died 10 Aug 1950 [Smithson stated this is a marker for his World War I service, but there is no record for him in *Maryland in the World War, 1917-1919.*]

PEARCE GRAVE SITE
Unnamed infant, son of Fred Pearce and Blanche Baldwin, of Clayton near Joppa, was stillborn on 15 Nov 1925 and his father buried him in the private cemetery of W. Groce as noted on infant's death certificate. [W. Groce has not yet been identified and the cemetery's location is undetermined.]

PHILLIPS CEMETERY
Identified as Aberdeen Proving Ground Private Cemetery P-4 by the U. S. Government, this cemetery at "Old Baltimore" is west of Old Baltimore Road on an unidentified lane about four miles from the mouth of Bush River and ¼ mile from the elbow of Romney Creek. See the binders of *Silent Sentinels of Aberdeen Proving Ground* (1999) at the Historical Society of Harford County in Bel Air, MD for tombstone images and further cemetery details. [Information

in brackets gleaned from comments in J. Crawford Neilson's Priestford Notebook, p. 38 (microfilm MS.613 at Maryland Historical Society) when he copied the markers in 1889.]

Phillips, William Pitt, died 20 Jul 1791 in his 11th year

Phillips, John Paca, died 27 Sep 1802, age 27 years, 2 months and 10 days

Phillips, James, Jr., died 10 Feb 1812, age 41 years and 10 days [He married Miss Wilmer and had an only child Martha who married William Paca. James' widow married second to Frank Dallam, of Baltimore, and they had several children.]

Phillips, James, died 14 Jun 1803 in his 63rd year

Phillips, Martha, wife of James Phillips and daughter of John and Elizabeth Paca, born 3 Feb 1744, married 25 Jun 1766, died 6 Mar 1829, having survived her husband 26 years.

PLATT'S HILL CEMETERY

A query submitted by Mrs. J. Nolan Callahan, of Baltimore, appeared in the *Head of Chesapeake Genealogical Register*, No. 3, January, 1978, p. 21. [Ed. Note: My attempts to locate this land tract and this cemetery have been unsuccessful.]

"Platt, Bayless, McConkey. Interested in locating the 'Platt's Hill' family cemetery near Darlington, Harford County, where members of these interrelated families are buried."

POTEET CEMETERY

An unidentified copyist stated this cemetery is located on a farm in the Fourth District, near Madonna, and the story of Elizabeth T. Poteet's death was that she was riding on the farm wagon and was killed by a piece of the wheel that flew off and hit her. The following Poteets are buried beside her:

Poteet, James, died 8 May 1854, age 70

Poteet, Elizabeth T., died 11 Dec 1817, age 8, daughter of James and Adeline Poteet

Poteet, Corbin, died 11 May 1847 in his 19th year

PRICE – TURNER CEMETERY
This cemetery is located in a patch of woods about 200 feet behind a house near the southwestern corner of Philadelphia and Clayton Roads. The markers were copied in 1985 by an unknown copyist and the cemetery was visited about 15-20 years later by Henry C. Peden, Jr. who found an additional marker with the letters "T. T." inscribed on it.

Price, Elizabeth, died 26 May 1846, age 62 years, 9 months and 21 days

Price, William, Sr., died 25 Dec 1853, age 69 years, 9 months and 16 days

Turner, William, 1781 – 26 Aug 1826

Turner, Mary Kimberly, died 29 Oct 1804, age 64 years, 8 months and 15 days

T. T., no dates [probably the grave site of Thomas Turner according to the late Mrs. Thirza Brandt who was a relative]

PRINGLE CEMETERY
In 1936 Thomas C. Hopkins, of Havre de Grace, reported that "the grave of Mark Pringle has been discovered on his former plantation, Bloomsbury, near Havre de Grace. The tomb gives the date of death as 1819, the deceased being 58

years of age. Alongside is the tomb of a daughter, Eliza, two years old. Mr. Pringle was a prominent citizen of Harford and a large landowner, and history relates that his large brick mansion was battered by the British cannon during the bombardment of Havre de Grace in 1812." [It was actually in May 1813. See *Bel Air Times*, 18 Dec 1936, and *Harford Democrat*, 25 Dec 1936. The location of this old family cemetery is presently unknown, that is, if it even still exists. Pringle's wife Catharine was also probably buried there.]

Pringle, Mark, 1761 – 6 Jan 1819
[Baltimore merchant; *Baltimore Patriot*, 11 Jan 1819]

Pringle, Eliza, 2 years old (no dates)

Pringle, Catharine, wife of Mark U. Pringle, died 4 Mar 1821
[*Baltimore American*, and *Baltimore Patriot*, 5 Mar 1821]

PYLE CEMETERY
This cemetery, located on the hill behind the old Ralph Pyle house on the west side of Walters Mill Road off Route 543, was still in existence in 1970, but the house was slated to be demolished in 1971. Two pictures of the old house and two broken grave stones in a nearby field can be found in *Pyles of Bishops Canning, England*, by Howard Thornton and Jane Weaver Pyle (1980), a copy of which is filed in the Library of the Historical Society of Harford County.

Pyle, Ralph, died 13 Jun 1803, age 77

Pyle, Sarah, died 16 Apr 1804, age 73, wife of Ralph Pyle

Pyle, Samuel, died 3 Oct 1792, age about 20 years (St. James Parish Records)

RAPHEL CEMETERY

This cemetery was located on what is now Aberdeen Proving Ground, but the remains have been removed to St. Stephen's Church at Bradshaw in Baltimore County. When Etienne (or Stephen) Raphel wrote his will in 1811 he stated, in part, "I wish to be buried with the greatest simplicity without pomp, ceremony, or any other escort than that of my wife and children, on my farm, situated in Harford County, called Quiet Lodge, between the two children whom I there lost and who were there interred. The only honors I am ambitious of are the sincere tears of my family will shed upon my tomb. If my wife wishes to cover it with a stone, let it be as modest as my life has been obscure, and let her engrave upon it an inscription which may be a lesson for my children." (Baltimore County Wills Book 9, pp. 131-138).

In 1972 Clarence V. Joerndt published *St. Ignatius, Hickory, And Its Missions* and (on page 120) he wrote about Quiet Lodge, the old Presbury family house, which Etienne J. Raphel purchased in 1799. "His body was interred upon the farm upon his death in 1811 as was that of Jane Elizabeth, his wife, who survived him several years. The Arsenal [i.e., Edgewood Arsenal, Aberdeen Proving Ground] has stated that the body of Etienne (and presumably also of Jane Elizabeth) was buried in a vault in a burial plot in about the middle of the aviation field. Eventually they were removed and re-interred in the cemetery of St. Stephen in Bradshaw at the extreme southeast corner. When this occurred has not been learned. The son Stephen J. probably lived at Quiet Lodge … It was in 1854 that he disposed of Quiet Lodge."

The following persons named Raphel are now buried in St. Stephen's Catholic Churchyard and were probably removed from the Quiet Lodge farm in Harford County before 1916.

58

[Information in brackets was added by Henry C. Peden, Jr. in 2015 in part from Vol. 2 of *Baltimore County Cemeteries* (1980) copied by Baltimore County Genealogical Society.]

[Raphel, Etienne also known as Stephen, was born 18 Mar 1754 at Marseilles in Provence, France, died between 6 May 1811 and 15 Jun 1811 – no tombstone]

Raphel, Jane Elizabeth, born 22 Aug 1770 on the Island of St. Lucia [No date of death on tombstone; her parents were Philip and Jane Fressonjat]

Raphel, Elizabeth, 1799, St. Lucia – 8 Dec 1811

Raphel, Stephen J., 23 Feb 1790 – 29 Jan 1872
[Raphel married Mary Ann Macatee in 1834, but there is no grave marker for her.]

Raphel – two stones are partly buried – S.L.R. – H.C.R.
[S.L.R. was probably Stephanie Louisa Juliet Raphel, and H.C.R. was probably Henrietta Maria Clotilda Charlotte Alexandrine Anne Raphel, two daughters of Etienne Raphel. Their grave markers were copied by the Baltimore County Genealogical Society in 1980.]

Small stones – Maria Eugenia Raphel, infant daughter, and -- -- [no name given], son of Eugene and Jeanette, died 21 Apr 1889, age 2 years and 7 months. [Markers were copied by the Baltimore County Genealogical Society in 1980.]

Raphel, Stephanie L., 11 Nov 1794, born on the Island of St. Eustatia, died 22 Jun 1855. [Marker was copied by the Baltimore County Genealogical Society in 1980.]

REASIN GRAVE SITE
Identified as Aberdeen Proving Ground Private Cemetery P-6 by the U. S. Government, this grave site is located off Cod

Creek Road about 400 feet south of Towners Point Road. See the binders of *Silent Sentinels of Aberdeen Proving Ground* (1999) at the Historical Society of Harford County in Bel Air, Maryland for a tombstone image and cemetery details. [Information in brackets below was added by Henry C. Peden, Jr. in 2015.]

Reasin, William D., died 16 May 1832, age 41
[William Dooley Reasin served in the War of 1812.]

RIGDON CEMETERY

This cemetery no longer exists, but it was once somewhere on a Rigdon farm in the late 1800s. Emory United Methodist Church Cemetery in the 5th District has two Rigdon grave markers that an unidentified copyist years ago indicated, "These stones were said to have been moved from a farm."

Rigdon, Elen(?), died 17 Mar 1849, age 59
Rigdon, William, died 4 Apr 1869, age 64

RODGERS CEMETERY

Churchville Presbyterian Church's Register of Deaths states "Roland Rogers" died on 30 Jul 1848 and was buried on his farm. In 2016 researcher Christopher T. Smithson stated that Rodgers' grave is at Mt Zion United Methodist Church and his tombstone is older than the church. Further investigation revealed that John and Mary Adams sold ½ acre for a school and place of worship in 1846 (school discontinued in 1858 and church dedicated in 1868). The Rodgers farm was on the north side of Churchville Road across from the church. The following were later moved and re-interred in the cemetery:

Rodgers, Sarah J. (1836-1838)
Rodgers, Rowland (1775-1848)
Rodgers, Catharine (1779-1855)
Rodgers, Elijah B. (1806-1861)

RUMSEY CEMETERY

A publication titled *The Church in Gunpowder Hundred* included this comment: "The Rumsey family burial ground lies in the northwest corner of the original three acre tract [where the original St. John's Church, now gone, once stood on Rumsey Island in present day Joppatowne], and in 1965, all that remained was part of the wall, which was then at ground level and one gravestone, that of Caroline B. Rumsey, who died June 8, 1846. This gravestone as recently as March 22, 1975, although lying flat, was only slightly damaged." In 2015 Henry C. Peden, Jr. and Jack L. Shagena, Jr. visited the site and only found Caroline's grave marker where the old family cemetery was once located. Adjacent to this burying ground was the church cemetery that today only contains the marker of David McCulloch, merchant in Joppa, who died on 17 Sep 1766, age 48. Nearby is a collection of small pieces of a few other grave markers, probably from the old church's cemetery, that had been molded together in cement and displayed in a small garden area. [Information in brackets below was added by Henry C. Peden, Jr. in 2015.]

Rumsey, Caroline B., died 8 Jun 1846

Rumsey, Benjamin, 6 Oct 1734 – 7 Mar 1808 [probably buried here – no marker]

Rumsey, Mary Hall, wife of Benjamin Rumsey [probably buried here – no marker]

Rumsey, Benjamin, Jr., 1775-1799 [probably buried here – son of Benjamin Rumsey – no marker]

Rumsey, John, 1780-1790 [probably buried here – son of Benjamin Rumsey – no marker]

RUTLEDGE CEMETERY

This cemetery is located on the east side of Madonna Road in the Nelson Mill Road area, two and one-half miles north of Jarrettsville on the Brick House farm that was owned by William Rutledge circa the 1950s. [Information in brackets below added by Henry C. Peden, Jr. in 2015.] The following information, in part, was copied many years ago and a copy was filed at the Historical Society of Harford County.

Row 1
Man 1820

Row 2
Rutledge, Augustena, died 6 Apr 1819, wife of Joshua Rutledge [Family records state she was born 18 Mar 1774.]

Rutledge, Joshua, son of the late Joshua Rutledge [who was] a Revolutionary Officer, died 22 Feb 1843 in his 20th [?] year. [Family records indicate he was born 15 Nov 1798.]

Row 3
Curry, Eliza, born in Kent, England, died 19 Dec 1824, age 33, wife of Israel Curry

Rutledge, Ruth, died 31 Jan 1817, age 71, wife of John

Rutledge. John, died 19 Aug 1800, age 47

Row 4
Unmarked stone

RUTLEDGE GRAVE SITE

The following burial information was gleaned from *The Whiteford Genealogy*, by Hazel Whiteford Baldwin (1992), pp. 317-318:

"Jacob Rutledge, son of Abraham Rutledge and Penelope Rutledge, born c1762, died 16 February 1815 and buried on farm property, Rutledge Road in Fallston, Maryland, married 1 April 1799 to Monica Wheeler, daughter of Ignatius Wheeler, Jr. and Henrietta (Neale) Smith ... The above three sons [John W., Ignatius and Abraham] of Jacob and Monica were orphaned and lived with uncle and aunt, Joshua and Augustine, at Brick House farm, Madonna and Nelson Mill Roads, Jarrettsville, Harford County. Joshua and Augustine are buried on the farm property."

"The Gateway," a booklet prepared by The Fallston-Upper Cross Roads Bicentennial Committee, states "The Rutledge farm owned today [1976] by J. C. Rutledge is still intact from its purchase about the time of the revolution. Abraham Rutledge purchased it as part of the 'Lord Baltimore Grant' ... Two graves are in the garden of the original house. One is of Abraham who requested that he not be taken off the land but be buried at home. Others in the family did not want to be buried there so it did not become a family plot."

RUTLEDGE GRAVE SITE

This burying ground is located in a wooded area near the southwest corner of Jerry's Road and Fawn Grove Road. Only two graves are enclosed within an iron fence, much neglected. [Henry C. Peden, Jr. and Jack L. Shagena, Jr. visited the site in 2010. The stone of Ariel Rutledge was very weathered and illegible for the most part. Her dates of birth and death have been gleaned from *Children of Mt. Amos*, by Gertrude J. Stephens (1992), page 80.]

Rutledge, Abraham (major), 9 Dec 1795 – 24 Jun 1875, son of Lt. Joshua Rutledge

Rutledge, Ariel Amos, 27 Mar 1816 – 12 Sep 1860, wife of Abraham Rutledge

SAPPINGTON CEMETERY

When the *Silent Sentinels of Aberdeen Proving Ground* was compiled by the U. S. Government in 1999 the following information was included as regards the Sappington family: "Spesutie Island was, at one time, apparently the home of several members of the Sappington family. A memorial marker has been erected at St Stephen's Episcopal Church Cemetery, MD Rte. 213 and MD Rte. 282 in Cecilton, Cecil County, Maryland, with the following inscription:

1695   1995

In memory of Nathaniel Sappington

- 1713

and his wife

Mary

Dedicated by the "Sappingtons of America"

on the 300th Anniversary of the Recording

of his presence in Maryland

Children of

Nathaniel & Mary

Nathaniel m Margaret Hartley

James m

Thomas m Mary Rutland

John m Sarah Sherbert

It was also stated by the U. S. Government in 1999: "There is no evidence, at present, of any Sappington Family grave markers on Spesutie Island."

SCHIPKE GRAVE SITE

In 2011 Leonard Laylon, Cemetery Records Chairman of the Historical Society of Harford County, found the following information in Holy Trinity Episcopal Church's burial records on pages 260-261, entry #60:

Jacquelyn F. Schipke, female, age 62 (birth 1935); last residence: Bel Air; death 3 July 1998; Place of Interment:

Bonita Farm, Darlington, 18 July 1998; Minister: McIntyre. [Another record states Jacquelyn was born on 29 Nov 1935]

The Aegis on 8 Jul 1968 also reported that Jacquelyn Schipke, of Bel Air, age 62, died 3 July 1998 at her home and was survived by her husband Roger W. Schipke, of Bel Air, a daughter Kimberly Schipke Boniface, of Darlington, two sisters and one brother. Arrangements by Schimunek Funeral Home.

SEWELL CEMETERY

In 1891 local historian George W. Archer (1824-1907) made the following comments in regards to this cemetery: "The Sewell graveyard [is] about 5 steps from the road leading from Abingdon to Harford Station. No fence between it and the road. The graveyard is substantially enclosed with a granite wall [and gate]. There are only two marked graves – at the head & foot of each is a rough granite block about 18 inches high, without letters or characters of any kind – probably[?] of Col. Sewell & wife. There are a few depressions in the enclosure – without any stone or board – about where the marks are in the plat [referring to his sketch]. A solitary tree (cedar) about 6 to 8 inches in diameter at the front stands within the enclosure near the S. E. corner ... overgrown with briers and weeds."

A further investigation by Henry C. Peden, Jr. in 2015 led to personal information from Howard K. McComas, Jr. and his cousin William Sewell that the family cemetery is now gone, probably as a result of the widening of Sewell Road many years ago. The bodies were re-interred in the cemetery at Cokesbury United Methodist Church in Abingdon. In that cemetery the Sewell family plot in Row 6, Lots 1 & 2, is marked with a large obelisk in the shape of a cross and inscribed with many names on all four sides of its base. The following persons were probably originally buried in the Sewell cemetery on Sewell Road, two of whom are noted in *The Aegis and Intelligencer*, and *Harford Democrat*, on 13 Aug 1869:

Sewell, Col. Charles Smith, 1779-1848

Sewell, Ann Catherine, 1783-1836, his wife

Sewell, Charles Smith, Jr., 1809-1832

Sewell, Edwin Augustus, 1818-1825

Sewell, C. K., 1861-1909

Sothern, Cornelia, 1759-1821, mother of Charles S. Sewell

Stake, Catherine, 1758-1822, mother of Catherine Sewell

Sewell, Septimus Davidge, 1822-1869

Sewell, Maria Louisa, 1832-1910, his wife, and infant son Bowie

Sewell, Jacob Keagy Smith, M.D., 1813-1840

Morsell, Ann Maria, 1810-1832, and infant daughter

Sewell, James Monroe, 1820-1869

SHIPLEY CEMETERY

In 1972 Clarence V. Joerndt published *St. Ignatius, Hickory, And Its Missions*. On pages 124-125 he included the three burials on Joshua Shipley's place near Black Horse Tavern. Joerndt stated that "The Joshua Shipley place was identified with reasonable certainty, but the home (perhaps a log cabin) is no longer standing ... Some 100 to 150 feet to the rear of

66

the home was the graveyard. This was confirmed by an elderly person who as a youngster played on the grounds and recalls the cemetery plot and the last tombstone that was there. Now there is nothing! The fact that the land contained a cemetery is known to relatively few – at least so one must believe – and a year or two ago when the location of the plot was pointed out, it was overgrown by a thriving field of corn." [It is interesting to note that no one named Shipley is known to have been buried in the Shipley Cemetery, which could possibly indicate that most grave markers, including Shipleys, were missing when Joerndt wrote his 1972 book.]

Fulwiler, Frances S., age about 21 years, buried 1 Jul 1835

Wire, Eve, age about 90, buried 1 Jul 1835

Doran, Margaret, buried 1 Jul 1835 [no age given]

SKINNER CEMETERY

This African American family cemetery is located in a wooded area between 622 and 624 Chapel Terrace in Havre de Grace. Due to its location to the north of the train tracks it is thought to have also been known as the B&O Cemetery and/or Zion Hill Cemetery. It was the site of the original St. James AME Church on Zion Hill in 1849 and "the first cemetery which is still there called the Skinner Cemetery," according to the late Mrs. Geraldine W. Cox, of Aberdeen, in 2001. The present St. James Cemetery is located next to the Mt. Erin Cemetery near Graceview Road. There were only a few tombstones in the Skinner Cemetery when they were copied by Reggie Bishop some years ago. Additional burials were found in a number of Harford County death certificates by Henry C. Peden, Jr. in 2015 and his research comments [in brackets] have been included in the listing that follows.

Skinner, Beulah, 12 Sep 1897 – 17 Sep 1914 [tombstone]

[Death certificate states Beulah Skinner was the daughter of Horace Skinner and Rose German.]

Skinner, Frances J., 1842 – 24 Dec 1920 [tombstone]
[Death certificate states Frances Skinner was about age 75 and the widowed daughter of James Legar and Mary Scott, but her tombstone indicated she was 78.]

Skinner, Henry, died – Nov 1918, age 68 [tombstone]
[Information from Bishop's transcription; Death certificate states Joseph H. Skinner died 5 Nov 1918, age about 68, and was married, son of Horace Skinner and Hattie Martin.]

Skinner, Sadie, 1 Oct 1882(?) – 28 Feb 1901 [tombstone]

Skinner, Sid(?) – illegible dates [Bishop indicated the tombstone needs rubbing.]

Skinner, Thomas G., died 18 Oct 1912, age 40 [tombstone]
[Death certificate states he was single and born 3 Dec 1874, the son of Sidney H. Skinner and Frances Leger, but it also states he was buried in St. James Cemetery.]

Skinner, Victoria, died 5 Aug 1887, age 2 years and 20 days [tombstone]

Skinner, Walter, died 17 Oct 1912, age 16 [tombstone]
[Death certificate states he was single, born 21 Jun 1896, the son of Horace Skinner and Rosa German, but it also states he was buried in St. James Cemetery.]

Skinner, William T. or E., died 15 Aug 1887, age 2 months and 15 days [tombstone]

Skinner, Willie, 1884 – 18 Jul 1907 [tombstone]
[Death certificate states William Skinner, son of J. T. Skinner and Lizzie Sorrell, was single and died at age 20

68

years, 6 months and 23 days, which would make his birth
date 26 Dec 1886, not 1884]

Christy, Emma, 5 Jul 1863 – 3 Apr 1920 [no marker]
[Death certificate states she was the daughter of Edward
Small and Frances Skinner.]

Christy, Harry, 5 Jun 1882 – 20 Dec 1914 [no marker]
[Death certificate states he was the son of John R. Christy
and Emma Small.]

Cole, Isaac, died 7 Dec 1921 (stillborn) [no marker]
[Death certificate states he was the son of Isaac Cole and
Ellen Lisby.]

Durbin, Ella Jane, 14 Jan 1865 – 29 Dec 1941 [no marker]
[Death certificate states she was the daughter of James H.
Leggar and Elin Myers.]

Durbin, Nathaniel, 10 Jul 1860 –1 Mar 1924 [no marker]
[Death certificate states he was the son of Stephen Durbin
and Celesta Skinner.]

Harris, Baby, 24 Jul 1946 – 26 Jul 1946 [no marker]
[Death certificate states he was the son of William Harris
and Marie Hawkins.]

Hawkins, Calvin, 27 Jan 1932 – 15 Feb 1935 [no marker]
[Death certificate states he was the son of James E. Hawkins
and Frances Skinner.]

Hawkins, Frances, 9 Jun 1911 – 30 May 1937 [no marker]
[Death certificate states she was the daughter of Henry
Skinner and Minnie Richardson.]

Hawkins, Irene, 14 Nov 1923 – 1 Mar 1937 [no marker]

[Death certificate states Irene Hawkins was the daughter of Ralph Hawkins and Ella Maddox.]

Hill, James, 8 Jan 1833 – 4 Mar 1911 [no marker]
[Death certificate states he was single and the son of Aquilla Hill; mother unknown.]

Jackson, James, born about 31 Jan 1902, Los Angeles – died 19 Jun 1948 [no marker]
[Death certificate states he was widowed laborer and there was no record of his parents.]

Martin, Mary, 1 Jun 1863 – 23 Jun 1911 [no marker]
[Death certificate states she was the daughter of John Rumsey and Harriet Kane.]

Samuels, Louise, 5 Sep 1923 – 17 Sep 1923 [no marker]
[Death certificate states she was the daughter of Arthur Samuels and Olivia Skinner.]

Skinner, Elizabeth, died 16 Feb 1920, age about 45 [but no marker; Death certificate states she was the daughter of James Sorrell and Rachel Armstead.]

Skinner, Horace S., 1 Jan 1867 – 30 Jun 1934 [no marker in Skinner Cemetery even though his death certificate states he was buried there, but in St. James Cemetery (next to Mt. Erin Cemetery) there is a marker for him and his wife Rosa G. Skinner]

Skinner, J. T., died 29(?) Sep 1904, under 4 weeks old [no marker in Skinner Cemetery and his death certificate did not indicate the place of burial in Havre de Grace; he was the son of J. T. Skinner and Lizzie Sorrell.]

Skinner, John T., died 20 May 1930, age about 63 [but no marker; Death certificate states he was the widowed son of Jacob Skinner; mother unknown.]

Skinner, Juanita, 5 Mar 1916 – 14 Aug 1916 [but no marker; Death certificate states she was the daughter of Teavre Tildon and Emma Skinner.]

Skinner, Lewis, died 5 Jul 1904, age 45 [but no marker; Death certificate states he was single and the son of John Skinner, mother unknown, and place of burial not indicated.]

Skinner, Marie, 5 May 1915 – 12 Oct 1918 [but no marker; Death certificate states she was the daughter of Harry Thompson and Annie Skinner.]

Skinner, Minnie, 1 Nov 1892 – 22 Sep 1927 [but no marker; wife of Henry Skinner; Death certificate states she was the daughter of John Richardson, mother unknown.]

Sorrell, Creswell, 30 Oct 1901 – 3 Nov 1918 [but no marker; Death certificate states he was single and the son of Willie Sorrell, mother unknown.]

Sorrell, William, 1 Aug 1879 – 6 Aug 1916 [but no marker; Death certificate states he was single and son of Edward Sorrell and Fannie Skinner.]

Stansbury, Clarence E., 31 Aug 1921 – 13 Apr 1924 [but no marker; Death certificate states he was single and son of Orie Stansbury and Emma Skinner.]

Wise, J. Henry, 29 Oct 1876 – 20 Jun 1924 [but no marker; Death certificate states he was the son of Daniel Wise and Mary Ellen Skinner.]

Wise, Mary Ellen, died 21 Dec 1926, age about 60 [but no marker; Death certificate states she was the daughter of Jack Skinner and Frances Legar.]

Wise, Milton, 2 Apr 1913 – 4 Oct 1913 [no marker here, but his death certificate states he was the son of Thomas Wise and Susie Pinion, buried in St. James Cemetery]

SLADE CEMETERY

Some years ago photocopies of pages from the family Bible of James A. Slade was donated to the Historical Society of Harford County by Patricia Czerniewski of the Baltimore County Genealogical Society. It mentioned the marriage of James W. Slade and Hannah McComas on 11 Dec 1813 and the marriage of James A. Slade and Louisa B. Slade on 18 Oct 1849, plus the following burials. It also indicated James Joshua Slade, son of James A. and Louisa Slade, was born 11 Aug 1850 on his father's farm near Little Creek, which gives some indication as to where this family burial ground may have been.

Slade, James W., father of James A. Slade, died 6 May 1849 and buried on the farm he owned, born 25 Jul 1793 (marker)

Slade, Hannah McComas, mother of James A. Slade, died 19 Nov 1877 and buried in the family burial ground, born 1796 (marker)

SLAVE CEMETERY

About 50-60 years ago local historian Joseph L. Hughes noted that the following slaves of Henry Michael were buried on Gravelly farm, but he listed no dates of death.

Eliza, born 3 Mar 1845
Ellen, born 12 Aug 1847
Nancy, born 17 May 1850
Fanny, born 20 Oct 1854

Tiny, born 18 Apr 1857
Ann, born 24 Jun 1861

SMITH CEMETERY

This family cemetery was once located at the rear of the Aberdeen Sales Barn on Route 22 in Churchville, but it and the sales barn no longer exist. It was described as having a "boarded fence, covered with lilies, many stones lying flat on the ground, sunken places in earth indicated many burials without stones, some graves marked with grey stones, size of cemetery about 50' x 100'." The markers have been moved to Smith's Chapel (date undetermined). [Information in brackets below was added by Henry C. Peden, Jr. in 2015.]

Coale, Sarah, died 23 May 1901, wife of Joseph R. Coale

Coale, Joseph, died 14 Jan 1864, age 56

Smith, William, 3 Mar 1770 – 17 Dec 1835

Smith, William, Jr., born [sic] 26 Jan 1807, age 1 week

Smith, Sally Virchworth, wife of William Smith (no dates) [The copyist misspelled her name as Sally March Worth, but records indicate it was spelled Virchworth; see Sallie Smith on the next page who appears to be the same person.]

Smith, Jane, 19 Aug 1804 – 7 Mar 1879

Smith, Nancy, 5 Dec 1793 – 10 Mar 1873

Smith, Margaret, 19 Feb 1802 – 21 Dec 1872

Smith, Harriett, 30 Dec 1798 – 24 Aug 1804

Smith, Sallie, 11 Sep 1769 – 9 Mar 1842 [see Sally Virchworth Smith above]

Coale, Louisa, died 26 Sep 1851, age 12 years and 5 months, daughter of Joseph and Sarah Ann Coale

Coale, John Reed, died 16 Feb 1818 [1848?], age 3 years and 4 months, son of Joseph and Sarah Ann Coale

SMITH – SAPPINGTON CEMETERY
(BLENHEIM CEMETERY)
This walled burying ground is located on property known as Blenheim (now part of the Bulle Rock housing development and golf course) that was once owned by Miss Inez H. Osborn (1880-1977). It is north of Oakington, near Havre de Grace. The land passed from the hands of the Smith family about 1831 when acquired by William Sappington, whose brother John K. Sappington enclosed the graveyard with a stone wall, and whose daughter Helen Matthews sold it to Miss Osborn's father Henry A. Osborn c1887. [Information in brackets below added by Henry C. Peden, Jr. in 2015.]

Smith, Sarah Knight, 8 Mar 1779 – 30 May 1828, wife of Paca Smith and daughter of James and Martha Phillips

Smith, Paca, 2 Dec 1779 – 25 Aug 1830, son of William and Susan Smith

Sappington, Dr. William, 3 Feb 1789 – 1 Dec 1849

Sappington, Amelia Jane, 14 Apr 1792 – 7 Feb 1843, wife of Dr. William Sappington and daughter of Henry and Hannah Ramsly(?)

Sappington, Dr. Richard, died 21 Apr 1824 in his 69th year, "my father"

74

Sappington, Mrs. Cassandra, born 14 May 1766(?), died 25 Sep 1852

Sappington, ---- [There may have been a child's grave between Richard and Cassandra Sappington as indicated by a copyist who stated "Child's grave not observed Nov 1971."]

Ramsay, Nathan, 12 Sep 1836 – 7 Nov 1864, colored, the faithful and honest servant of Dr. J. K. Sappington [His marker is located outside of the walls of this cemetery.]

Howard, Luther, died 6 Dec 1942, faithful Negro servant of the Osborn's [His death certificate stated Luther was age 65 and he was buried in Osborne's Cemetery. His grave marker is located outside of the walls of this cemetery.]

SMITHSON CEMETERY
This cemetery was once located near the southeast corner of Telegraph Road and Eden Mill Road near St. Paul's Church, about 6 miles from Pylesville, but it is no longer in existence. Christopher T. Smithson, of Darlington, MD, stated in 2003 that he has the tombstone of Capt. John Taylor Smithson. "This cemetery was on the Knopp property which is at the corner of Telegraph and Eden Mill Roads ... His home, which was a log cabin, was torn down in the 1970s. The present house is over 100 years old." Smithson also provided this information about the Smithsons buried in this cemetery:

Smithson, John Taylor, died 16 Jun 1857 [He was a captain and a Defender of Baltimore in the War of 1812 (as inscribed at the bottom of his marker) and he was born 20 Jun 1792]

Smithson, Hannah, died 12 Nov 1840, age 45, wife of John
Smithson, James Luther, died 20 Mar 1856, age 25
Smithson, Thomas Martin, died 22 Mar 1856, age 22

SMITHSON CEMETERY

This cemetery was once located on Telegraph Road about a mile west of and on the same side of the road as the Wright farm (near St. Paul's Church) and on the opposite side of the road from the Smithson Cemetery cited above. It no longer exists, but Christopher T. Smithson, of Darlington, MD, in 2015 stated there was at least one burial in this family cemetery and probably a few more unidentified. He also indicated Thomas Smithson's marker had been found by railroad workers many years ago and it somehow ended up at Silbaugh's Monuments in Shrewsbury, PA.

Smithson, Thomas, of Daniel, 1 Mar 1785 – 29 Oct 1859
    [War of 1812 soldier]
Smithson, Cassandra Poteet, c1781 – 1850s, wife of Thomas
    [most likely buried here]

SMITHSON – FARNANDIS CEMETERY
(Col. Dorsey's Graveyard)

This cemetery no longer exists, but was once located near what is now the south side of Townsend Lane, just west of Maitland Street and north of the old Homestead and Bel Air United Methodist Church. In 1901 Walter W. Preston wrote in his *History of Harford County, Maryland* (page 221): "Just outside the southeasterly limits of Belair [sic], and along the division line between the Fulford and Homestead farms, is the old graveyard of the Smithson and Farnandis families. After diligent search the headstone over the grave of William Smithson was found, nearly sunk in the ground and quite hidden by the weeds and grass. On the tomb is this inscription: In Memory of William Smithson, who departed this life January 17, 1809, aged 64 years."

In 1870 Charles B. Coale (born 1807), formerly of Harford Co., then living in Abingdon, VA, wrote his recollections of

Harford County in a series of letters called "Glimpses From the Past" and they were published in *The Aegis* newspaper. Dr. George W. Archer abstracted the following information: "Billy Mills was the village barber [Bel Air]. He was also a tailor. He followed his affianced to the grave and they sleep side by side in Col. Dorsey's Graveyard in the Northeast corner of the orchard." According to researcher Christopher T. Smithson this was the Smithson-Farnandis Cemetery. *Our Harford Heritage*, by C. Milton Wright, p. 407 states, in part: "Born in Baltimore in 1817, Henry D. Farnandis was the son of Walter ... His mother was Mary Dorsey Farnandis, daughter of [Col.] Henry Dorsey, whom for many years was Clerk of the Circuit Court of Harford County ... [Farnandis] died in 1900 ... buried in Greenmount Cemetery in Baltimore." [Also see *Harford Historical Bulletin No. 14*]

In 1886 Mrs. Elijah B. Rogers, of Baltimore, wrote a letter in which she recalled Bel Air's residents in 1814. She stated Thomas and Billy Mills were tailors and boarded in a house two doors from Thomas Hays' store. "Billy was a butt for all the young folks; he was short and quite corpulent."

In the 1820 Harford County Census is enumerated William Mills, aged between 25 and 44, with one white female. This was in all likelihood Billy Mills and his wife. He is not listed in the 1830 census and no other records have been found to determine vital information. It appears they died by 1830.

SPENCER CEMETERY

These graves, located on the Worthington Brothers' farm on Rock Run Road near Rock Run United Methodist Church, were copied by an unidentified copyist circa 1970 who stated they were the children of John Walter Spencer and his wife Rebecca Keen.

Spencer, Herman, 1821 – 9 Nov 1839

Spencer, Mary Ann, 23 Sep 1833 – 1835

ST. CLAIR CEMETERY

Some time before 1983 Mrs. Margaret S. Bishop copied this cemetery. It is located at 3940 Old Federal Hill Road about a mile from Cooptown on a farm then owned by R. Melvin Moore (since deceased). The property was formerly owned by James Oscar Moore and before that it was owned by John St. Clair and his wife Elizabeth Ann Moore.

St. Clair, William, died 24 Mar 1819 in his 67th year

St. Clair, Hannah, died 25 Jan 1845, age 75

St. Clair, James S., died 18 Mar 1886 in his 77th year

St. Clair, Elizabeth, died 2 Feb 1884, age 80 (86?)

Slade, James S., died 5 Jun 1858 (1853?) in his 30th year

Slade, Stephen, died 3 Jan (Feb?) 1855 in his 27th year

Slade, John L., died 18 Apr 1855 in his 24th year

Slade, Priscilla, died 5 Jun 1852 in her 39th year

Slade, Stephen, died 29 Mar 1846, age 64

St. Clair, Caroline, 4 Jan 1818 – 23 Sep 1886

St. Clair, Elizabeth, died 15 Apr 1892

Goldwell, Margaret, died 7 May 1849, age 75

STANSBURY CEMETERY

This cemetery is located on top of a hill behind the mansion above Eden Mill and Deer Creek on Eden Mill Road. In 2009 Henry C. Peden, Jr. and Jack L. Shagena, Jr. visited the site and found an elegant iron entrance gate, but the cemetery was no longer enclosed. [Information in brackets below was added by Henry C. Peden, Jr. in 2015.]

Stansbury, Col. Isaac, died 2 Feb 1865 in his 76th year [Isaac was born 28 Jun 1788 and was a private in the War of 1812.]

Stansbury, James, died 28 Dec 1879 in his 62nd year [James operated Eden Mill, formerly known as Stansbury's Mill.]

Stansbury, Mary, died 17 Feb 1900 in her 82nd year, wife of James Stansbury [Mary Susannah Smithson married James Stansbury in Baltimore in 1847.]

Stansbury, Isaac William, died 1857 [illegible], age 3 years and 10 months

STANSBURY CEMETERY

The Harford County death certificate of William Henry Stansbury, an African American who lived at Cole, near Michaelsville and Spesutia Island, stated he was the son of Peter Stansbury and Harriet Lisbey. It also indicated that William was buried at "Home Private Graveyard" by G. Osborn & Sons, Undertakers, Perryman, MD. The cemetery no longer exists, but his parents and perhaps other family members could have also been buried here.

Stansbury, William Henry, 30 Dec 1832 – 6 Dec 1911

STEPHENSON CEMETERY

Notes written by "M. R. B., 1979" stated the following: "Stephenson Burying Ground – Site – No fences, No stones?

'Lost from sight' according to Jennette Parker's notebooks (1933-34) but the 1ˢᵗ Rock Run Meeting House was erected on pt. of burial ground parcel (1933-4 Notebooks). The present <u>memorial</u> on the site is a bit <u>S</u> of present Susq. St. Park Campground entrance <u>E</u> side Craigs Corner road approx. 1 mi. <u>N</u> of present Church bldg. @ apex of junction Craigs Corner Rd. & Rock Run Road @ 'Garland.'"

STOKES – HUFF CEMETERY

This old cemetery, located on the east side of Wilson Road about .2 mile south of Mill Green Road, was copied many years ago at which time the unidentified copyist stated it was in terrible condition. Some have called it the Wilson Road Quaker Cemetery. Maryland Historical Trust (HA-889) circa 1970 mistakenly called it the Wilson Family Graveyard and gave some different information {as shown below in braces}. The last two markers listed (Scarborough and Hall) were gleaned from *Historic Graves of Maryland and the District of Columbia*, by Helen W. Ridgely (1908) which also listed Hannah Stokes, but not others as shown below. [Information in brackets below added by Henry C. Peden, Jr. in 2015.]

Stokes, Hannah, died 28 Feb 1826, age 79 years, 10 months and 26 days, wife of Joseph Stokes {MHT HA-889 stated "Hannah Stokes d. 1825 at 79 yrs."}

Stokes, Joseph, died 23 Mar 1828, age 79
{MHT HA-889 stated "Joseph Stokes d. 1828 at 78 yrs."}

Scarborough, William T., died 22 Apr 1824, age 1 month
{MHT HA-889 did not list this marker.}

Barclay, John, died May 1833, age 93
{MHT HA-889 stated "John Barclay d. 1832"}

Forwood, Eliza., died 6 Jan 1837, age 32
{MHT HA-889 did not list this marker.}

Huff, Hannah H., Aug 1811 – 22 Jan 1876
{MHT HA-889 did not list this marker.}

Stone initialed D. S.
{MHT HA-889 did not list this marker.}

Huff, ----, broken stone, 1851
{MHT HA-889 did not list this marker.}

Stone initialed M. B.
{MHT HA-889 did not list this marker.}

Scarborough, Daniel, died 23 Jan 1834, age 13 [name was misspelled as Dan Scarbrouch]
{MHT HA-889 and another unidentified copyist did not list this marker.}

Hall, Hannah, died 11 Oct 1832, age 59 years, 2 months and 26 day, wife of Rice J. Hall
{MHT HA-889 and another unidentified copyist did not list this marker.}

Wood, Joy {MHT HA-889 listed this marker, without dates} [but no other copyist listed it].

STUMP CEMETERY

This large cemetery, once owned by the prominent Stump family, later owned circa the 1960s and 1970s by John T. Gardner and now part of Susquehanna State Park, is located near Craig's Corner on the north side of the road leading from Rock Run United Methodist Church to Stafford Bridge. The tombstones were copied by various Harford County historians in the early years, including George W. Archer circa the 1890s and Joseph Lee Hughes circa the 1950s. [A few discrepancies have been noted and some comments were added in brackets below by Henry C. Peden, Jr. in 2015.]

The following inscription is written in slate on top of the wall of the cemetery gate: John Stump, 1st founder of family in Md., married Cath. Bakem [Bakerin], 11 Nov 1726, Old Christ Church, Phila., Pa., where record preserved, died 1747 in Cecil on his land entitled "Stump's Fancy" near mouth of Susquehanna [Cath. Bakem or Bakerin was Catherine Baker]

Footstone H. C. S. (large marker broken and face down)

Stump, Samuel C., died 13 May 1854 in his 62nd year

Stump, Hannah, died 4th month, 19 [day], 1872 [her name appeared on one list, but not on another]

Stump, Thomas C., 8 Feb 1794 – 12 Feb 1858 [9?] [his name appeared on one list, but not on another]

Stump, Ann, "his wife unmarked" [her name appeared on one list, but not on another]

Stump, William, died 26 Jul 1831 in his 67th year

Stump, Duckett, 15 Aug 1775 – 4 Jan 1869, wife of William Stump of Henry & Rachel and daughter of Thomas & Mary Cooper of York Co., Pa.

Boyd, ----, died 13 Dec 1838, son of Stephen & Eliza Boyd

Hoopman, Peter, died 17 Jan 1840, age 79

Hoopman, Mary [C.], died 7 Jun 1827, age 30, consort of Peter Hoopman

Stump, Henry C., died 1 Aug 1872 in 66th year [his name appeared on one list, but not on another]

Holloway, Hugh S., 20 Jan 1813 – 29 Jun 1868 [his name appeared on one list, but not on another]

Holloway, Hester Ann, 24 Oct 1816 – 28 Sep 1880, wife of Hugh S. Holloway [appeared on one list, but not on another]

Dever, John H., died 5 Feb 1815, age 2 years, 4 months and 24 days

Row 2
Stump, Thomas C., 8 Feb 1794 – 12 Feb 1858 (or 1859)

Stump, Ann Kelly, died 26 Oct 1848, wife of Thomas Cooper Stump and daughter of John Kelly of York, Pa.

Stump, John Kelly, 9 Oct 1837 – 9 Feb 1862, son of Thomas C. Stump

Stump, William Henry, 15 Sep 1841 – 19 Feb 1865

Stump, Mary Ann, 12 Aug 1839 – 17 Apr 1865, wife of Judge Frederick Stump of Perry Point [Her tombstone states she died 17 May 1865, but *The Aegis and Intelligencer*, 21 Apr 1865, states Mary, wife of Frederick, died 17 Apr 1865 at *Evergreen* in Harford Co.]

Stump, Frederick (Judge), 17 Mar 1837 – 12 Sep 1901, son of John & Mary Alicia Stump
[His tombstone states he died 11 Sep 1901, but *The Aegis and Intelligencer*, 13 Sep 1901, states Frederick died "yesterday" which would have been 12 Sep 1901.]

83

Stump, Henry Arthur, 13 Feb 1857 at Perry Pt. – 10 Feb 1934 in the City of Baltimore, son of John & Alicia Stump of Perry Point

Riegel, Carrie T., 17 Feb 1863 – 24 Jan 1935, wife of Henry Arthur Stump and daughter of Jacob & Eliz. Theresa Riegel of Philadelphia

Stump, Augustine Herman, 31 May 1893 – 31 May 1958, Md. 1st Lt., 2nd Cavalry, WW I

Two more gravestones buried in the ground [sic].

Bageley, Samuel H., died 17 Apr 1851 in his 59th year

Wilson, Henry S., died 30 [20] Oct 1850 in his 26th year

Wilson, Christopher, 25 Feb 1792 – 23 Mar 1876

Wilson, Mary, died 5 Dec 1868 in her 75th year

Wilson, Hetty, died 19 Jul 1844 in her 50th year [her name appeared on one list, but not on another]

Row 3
Allen, ----, infant son of E. M. & Sallie E. Allen, died – Dec 1877

Wilson, William H., 26 Feb 1826 – 26 [25] Jun 1850 [Different day on different lists, but Churchville Presbyterian Church Register indicates he died 25 Jun 1850.]

Wilson, William, died 23 Sep 1840 in his 54th year [William Wilson served as a private in the War of 1812.]

Wilson, Rachel, 6 Jan 1786 – 17 Jul 1873

Price, Margaret G., 20 Aug 1818 (31 Jan 1848) – 11 (or 14) Sep 1855, daughter of John H. & Mary Price [George W. Archer indicated her correct birth date is 31 Jan 1848 and her correct date of death is 14 Sep 1855.]

Price, Mary, 9 Aug 1810 (1840) – 20 Aug 1818 (1848), daughter of John H. & Mary Price [George W. Archer indicated the correct years are born 1840 and died 1848.]

Price, Grace, 28 Nov 1810 – 20 Apr 1836, wife of John H.

Price, Mary, died 15 Jan 1831, aged 3 [5?] months, 21 days

Price, David E., 25 Dec 1770 – 29 Jul 1810

Ritchie, Jane, died 21 Jul 1878 in her 73rd year

Stump, Sarah Biays, 26 Dec 1797 – 19 May 1876, widow of John Wilson Stump

Stump, Mary B., died 1826 [on one list, but not on another]

Stump, Mary B., died 21 Nov 1881, age 55

Row 4
Archer, John [M.D.], 9 Oct 1777 – 27 [21] May 1830, distinguished for Professional Genius, Private Virtues

Archer, Ann, 29 Jan 1786 – 19 Aug 1867, wife of Dr. John

Stump, John, born in Cecil Co., died 11 [14] Feb 1816 at Stafford, age 63 years, 8 months and 9 days

Stump, Cassandra, 13 Jun 1762 – 26 Aug 1846, wife of John Stump, Jr.

Stump, Herman, 13 Aug 1798 at Stafford – 13 Mar 1881

Archer, John S., 16 Jul 1815 – 31 Aug 1835 [his name appeared on one list, but not on another]

Archer, Marian, 22 Oct 1825 – 12 Aug 1827 [her name appeared on one list, but not on another]

Stump, William, of John, died 28 Mar 1821 in his 39th year

Williams, James, 8 Nov 1774, Worcester Co., MD – 10 Mar 1838, Harford Co.

Williams, William, died – Oct 1822, age 2 years

Stump, John Wilson, 23 Feb 1792 – 21 Oct 1862 and [probably] his children:
      Stump, James Biays, 17 Dec 1815 – 4 Dec 1839
      Stump, Mary Biays, 18 Sep 18— - 23 Sep 18—
      Stump, Margaret Ann, 22 May 18— - 29 May 18—
      Stump, Jane, 10 Sep 18— - 19 Aug 18—
      Stump, William, 7 Dec 1829 – 15 Aug 1862
[The names and dates above are from a slab (3x6) over John W. Wilson's grave.]

Row 5
Stump, William Henry [M.D.], 22 Nov 1808 – 27 Sep 1879

Stump, Reuben, died 8 May 1841 in his 76th year

Stump, Margaret, died 15 Oct 1870 in her 86th year, wife of Reuben Stump

Harlan, Margaret, daughter of Jeremiah and Esther Harlan (no dates)

Harlan, Jeremiah (no dates)

Harlan, Esther, 9 Sep 1774 – 23 Mar 1861 [1864?], wife of Jeremiah Harlan

Harlan, Hannah, 9 Sep 1807 – 9 Aug 1872, daughter of Jeremiah & Esther Harlan

Harlan, Henry S., 18 Oct 1801 – 13 Jun 1888, son of Jeremiah & Esther Harlan

Row 6
Evans, Hannah Stump, died 14 Jul 1827, age 14 months, daughter of L. H. & Rachel S. Evans

Stump, John, of Henry, 11 Aug 1756 – 18 Nov 1828

Stump, Hannah, died 10 [20?] Nov 1824 in her 63rd year, wife of John Stump

Stump, Hannah, 21 Jul 18— - Sep 1839, daughter of John & Mary Alicia Stump

Stump, Henry (Judge), of Perry Point and Baltimore, 28 Dec 1795 – 29 Nov 1865

Stump, Pauline, 1842 – 18 Apr 1907, daughter of Judge Henry Stump

Unknown Graves on a list by George W. Archer (c1890):
Stump, John II, died 1796

Stump, Henry, died 1814

Stump, Rachel, died 1820, wife of Henry

Stump, Henry II, died 1815

Smith, Hugh, died 1839

Smith, Mary, died 1845

Carter, Hannah(?) [sic]

Stump, Elizabeth, of Henry, died 1802

Stump, John (of Stafford John), d. y. [died young]

Stump, Herman (of Stafford John), d. y. [died young]

Stump, Cassandra (of Stafford John), d. y. [died young]

Stump, Judge Henry III, died 1865 [he is also listed above]

Smith, John, of Joseph & Mary, d. y. [died young] c1800

Stump, Rachel C., 1st of [sic] William & Duckett, died 1801

Smith, Hugh, of Thomas & Hannah, d. y. [died young] 1820

Stump, Hannah, of John & Mary Alicia, d. y. [died young; she is also listed above] 1829

Dever, Robert [no dates]

Dever, Elizabeth (probably "E.D. 1828")

Dearholt, Nancy, her mother, died about 1821 and 2 children [no names, no dates]

Unknown Graves on another list by George W. Archer:
[As listed in order after the grave of Jane Ritchie above.]

Unknown (adult)

Unknown (adult)

Unknown (adult)

Unknown (1 stone, probably adult)

Unknown (child)

Unknown (1 stone)

Unknown (grave 3½ feet long; probably the leg of Peter Hoopman which was amputated)

E. D. 1828 [also appeared on the other list above]

Unknown (adult)

Unknown (adult; a child apparently buried in same grave at a later date)

Unknown (adult)

Unknown (grave 4½ feet long; a child)

Unknown (grave 5 feet long; a child)

Unknown (grave 4 feet long; a child)

Unknown (adult)

Unknown (adult)

Unknown (adult)

Unknown (adult)

Unknown (grave 5 feet long; a child)

Unknown (grave 5 feet long; a child)

Unknown (1 stone)

Unknown (adult)

Unknown (adult)

Unknown (grave 3 feet long; a child)

Unknown (child)

TAYLOR GRAVE SITE

This burial place was located on the south shore of Otter Point Creek, near Edgewood, north of Frey's Road, and only one tombstone remained there in 1987. An email message dated August 22, 2010 from Glenn Randers-Pehrson to Christopher T. Smithson regarding John Taylor, who was a Signer of the Bush Declaration in 1775, resulted in this information: "When we moved here in 1985 there was a small Taylor graveyard in the cornfield near our house. Around the early '90s the cornfield got developed, and the stones were bulldozed into a gully and buried with fill dirt. We did record the one or tombstones that were legible in 1985 and provided the information to the Harford County Genealogical Society for their cemetery records collection. I don't remember the exact location now. It was somewhere in the field between present-day Ebbtide Drive and Otter Creek Road, west of Frey's Road in Edgewood." [The relationship, if any, between John Taylor, the Signer, and the James Taylor buried in Edgewood is undetermined.]

Taylor, James, died 17 Apr 1816 in his 47th year

TAYLOR GRAVE SITE

The Harford County death certificate of "Baby Taylor," son of Virginia Taylor and Charles Laurie, states he was a five-month premature birth on 12 Dec 1937 and was buried at his mother's home in Bel Air by the father. The exact location was not given.

TAYLOR CEMETERY

The Aegis and Intelligencer reported on 2 Jul 1880 that Joseph Taylor, a brother of John Taylor, died on Tuesday [22 Jun 1880] and was buried on Wednesday afternoon in the family burying ground on Henry L. Taylor's farm. The cemetery was located next to the *Wood's Rest* farm owned by John Taylor, about three miles from Boothby Hill, now part of Aberdeen Proving Ground. It was also reported that the funeral procession had just left the graveyard when John Taylor's barn, only a short distance off, was consumed by fire. [In 1999 the U. S. Government took pictures of the tombstones and compiled *The Silent Sentinels of Aberdeen Proving Ground*. This family graveyard was not included.]

THOMAS – WARD CEMETERY

In 2015 Christopher T. Smithson, of Darlington, MD, stated there was a Thomas family cemetery on Walters Mill Road and possibly buried there were William Thomas, John Thomas, and Betty Thomas Smith, wife of Eli Smith. The will of William Thomas was written on 28 Dec 1820 and he stated, in part, "I further will that my executor apply ten dollars of my estate to the express purpose of enclosing the ancient burying ground that is in the old orchard on Joseph Ward's plantation." He also mentioned his siblings James Thomas, John Thomas, Jane Ward, Elizabeth Smith, and Hannah Ecoph [Ecoff]. It appears, therefore, that this was a burying ground for the Thomas and Ward families. William Thomas owned the land known as *John's Inheritance* that was located "on the public road leading from William Pyle's saw mill to Martin Grafton's." Thomas also bequeathed ten dollars to Stephen Rigdon to be applied towards the erection of a Baptist meeting house at Rock Ridge. [Harford County Will Book SR No. 1, pp. 238-239]. It is likely that early members of the Thomas and Ward families were buried in this cemetery that was considered "ancient" in 1820. William Thomas was probably one of them, but the Joseph Ward mentioned in William's will is buried at Deer Creek United Methodist Church.

TODD GRAVE SITE
An informative article about the old Wilson Cemetery on Windmill Hill Farm, titled "In Memoriam," was written by Peter Jay and printed in the *Sunday Sun* on 4 Apr 1993. In it he also mentioned George Todd had died on Holland Island in 1908 and was buried there.

TOLLY CEMETERY
Some records indicate that there was a Tolly burying ground somewhere in northwestern Harford County, near Taylor, in the late 1800s, but it probably no longer exists and nothing further is known about it except the following two burials [sources are cited in brackets below].

Tolly, James Walter, died 30 Mar 1887, age 81 years, 2 months and 14 days [St. James' Parish, My Lady's Manor, Funeral Records stated he was "buried in the home burial place in Harford County, St. James' Parish." In *The Aegis and Intelligencer*, 1 Apr 1887, it was reported he died at the residence of his son Joseph A. Tolly, near Taylor.]

Tolly, ----, child of Joseph Tolly, died circa 21 Aug 1882 [Edmund G. Kurtz Funeral Home Ledger, 1844-1883, page 79, on 21 Aug 1882, stated, "Joseph Tolly – child. Buried from Tollys. Buried at family burying ground on the farm."

TRAGER CEMETERY

Identified as Aberdeen Proving Ground Private Cemetery P-8 by the U. S. Government, this cemetery is located on Small Arms Range Road about one-quarter mile south of the intersection of Old Baltimore Road and Palmer Road. See the binders of *Silent Sentinels of Aberdeen Proving Ground* (1999) at the Historical Society of Harford County in Bel Air, MD for tombstone images and further cemetery details. At that time Jon Harlan Livezey, Esq. indicated a note (and also some marker photographs) at the Historical Society of Harford County stated that this cemetery was near the former house of Oscar Johnson (now gone).

Trager, John W., 15 Nov 1813 – 12 Aug 1847, son of William and Sarah Ann Trager

Trager, Sarah Ann, died 20 Sep 1825, age 52, consort of William Trager

Stone fragment [information missing] – years and 9 months

Stone fragment Will— died 25 May 1855, age 76 [probably William Trager]

Headstone, top missing [stone broken off at ground level]

Partial stone, broken, Dearest Mo--- [and a short poem]

W. L. 1807 [This is in all likelihood William Lester, died 12 May 1807, age 51]

TREADWAY CEMETERY

This cemetery was mentioned in a book titled *Treadway and Burket Families*, by William E. Treadway in 1951. On pp. 23-24 he stated Thomas Treadway was born about 1679, died in 1782 (over 100 years old), and "he is buried in the

Old Treadway Graveyard at Madonna, Harford County, Maryland. The legal title to the land upon which this cemetery is located was, in 1899, in John Thomas Cathcart, his great-great-grandson. On January 26, 1761 he married Mrs. Mary Gittings … [who died] … on May 31, 1779." She is probably buried here as well. In 2011 Wes Herrmann, who lived at 4102 Harford Creamery Road, stated in an email to Henry C. Peden, Jr. that his wife Betsy told him that "his daughter Charlotte and Layne Hockaday were riding years ago behind Nancy Hockaday's house on Norrisville Road near the Madonna intersection and discovered a very old hidden graveyard." Whoever rests there, however, is yet to be undetermined. He also stated "Daniel Treadway and his wife Sarah Norris were buried at their homestead either on *Houndslow Heath* or *Tredway's Hope*." Records show that Daniel was born 22 Nov 1724 and died 25 May 1810, and his wife Sarah Norris Treadway was born in 1727.

UTIE – BOOTHBY CEMETERY
In 1908 Helen W. Ridgely published *Historic Graves of Maryland and the District of Columbia* (p. 95) and wrote, "There is an old graveyard at Level between Mosquito creek and the Narrows, where some of the Uties and Boothbys were buried. In fact, throughout the whole region below the Old Post road from Havre de Grace or the Lower Ferry, to the Patapsco River Necks, family graveyards were once known to abound." The area she is referring to in Harford County is now the U. S. Government's Aberdeen Proving Ground. However, no graves of members of the Utie and Boothby families who settled at Boothby Hill and on Spesutia Island were found when the government surveyed the area in 1999.

WEBSTER CEMETERY
This cemetery is located about five miles southeast of Bel Air on Route 543 (Fountain Green Road) and about a half mile from Creswell. It is situated on the *Broom's Bloom* land

tract that is owned by the Dallam family. The cemetery is near the edge of a cow pasture about 100 yards north of the barn and next to a housing development. The adjoining farm to the south is *Mount Adams*, a tract once owned by Capt. John Adams Webster of War of 1812 fame. [For additional information about the captain see *The Aegis*, 13 Jul 1877.]

Webster, James Biays, M.D., 24 Nov 1828 – 12 Aug 1890, son of Capt. John A. and Rachel Webster

Webster, Susan A., 27 Feb 1830 – 3 Oct 1895, daughter of John A. and Rachel Webster

Webster, Rachel, died 3 Oct 1869, age 72, wife of Capt. John A. Webster and daughter of Joseph and Elizabeth Biays

Webster, Isaac R., died at Malvern Hill [Virginia] on 1 Jul 1862 of camp fever, in his 23rd year

Bond, Sandie Webster, 17 Sep 1837 – 11 Jun 1875, wife of Frank A. Bond [Records indicate this was Rachel Cassandra Webster who was nicknamed Sandie.]

Webster, John Adams, died 4 Jul 1877, age 90; inscribed on the reverse of his marker: "Captain Webster began life as a sailor when fourteen years old. In 1812, he served as Captain under Commodore Barney; also in the flotilla on the Chesapeake in 1813 and 1814; and was in the same command at the battle of Bladensburg Aug. 24, 1815 in which his horse was shot under him. After the battle he marched to Baltimore with his sailors and by Gen. Smith's order took command of the SIX GUN BATTERY from which on the night of the 13 of September 1814 he attacked the enemy's barges and defeated them with great loss, thus rendering most efficient service in the defense of Baltimore. On Nov. 22, 1819 he was commissioned Captain in the U. S. R. N. and in May 1846 commanded a fleet of eight vessels in cooperation with the army and navy in the War with Mexico. He took part in twenty engagements by land and sea, was twice wounded and at the time of his death was senior Captain in the Revenue Service. In every position he served his country faithfully, gallantly and efficiently. And died a Christian."

Barney, Mrs. Margaret, died 31 Aug 1829, age 53 years and 5 months, consort of John H. Barney

Waltham, Mrs. Alice A., died 7 Dec 1858 in her 80th year, daughter of Sam and Margaret Webster and relict of the late Clement Waltham of Harford County, Md.

WESLEY GRAVE SITE

Identified as Aberdeen Proving Ground Private Cemetery P-9 by the U. S. Government, this grave is located on Small Arms Range Road about one-quarter of a mile south of the intersection of Old Baltimore Road and Palmer Road and just south of the Trager Cemetery. See the binders of *Silent Sentinels of Aberdeen Proving Ground* (1999) at the Historical Society of Harford County in Bel Air, MD for the tombstone image and further cemetery details.

Wesley, Jacob, died 8 Sep 1870, age 38

WESTWOOD CEMETERY
(see Coale Cemetery)

WHITAKER CEMETERY

A picture of a marker (slab) with names of members of the Whitaker family appeared in *The Aegis* on 13 May 1973 with this caption: "Strange Step – When workers demolished a house, estimated to be thirty or forty years old, at the Heritage Woods construction site on Moores Mill road last week, they found this burial plot marker which had been used as a back step. The stone noted the resting place of one Joshua Whitaker who died in 1818 at the age of 57; his wife, and several children, apparently including another Joshua, who died in 1861, at age 66. The marker was erected, but no one knows originally where, by A. B. and O. M. Whitaker in 1899. The marble block is about three feet long, 18 inches wide and 18 inches thick, and weighs 500 to 800 pounds." Whatever became of it is not known at the present time. The following people were listed on the marker:

Joshua Whitaker, died 1818, age 57

Ruth Howard Whitaker, his wife [no dates]

Aquila Whitaker [no dates]

Nancy West [no dates]

Martha Kean [no dates]

Susan Whitaker [no dates]

Martha Whitaker [no dates]

Ruth Hawkins [no dates]

Joshua Whitaker, died 1861, age 66

WHITTINGTON GRAVE SITE

The Harford County death certificate of an unnamed African American infant and the stillborn son of Andrew Thomas Whittington and Louisa Dorsey, stated he "was dead at least a week before birth" as reported by Dr. A. F. Van Bibber on 3 Nov 1914. The baby was buried by his father at Doxen's Corner, a rural area near Bel Air, where the family lived.

WILLIAMS BROTHERS GRAVE SITE

These two graves have been identified as Aberdeen Proving Ground Private Cemetery P-P.I. by the U. S. Government. They are located on Poole's Island south of the lighthouse in the northwestern corner of the island. See the binders of *Silent Sentinels of Aberdeen Proving Ground* (1999) at the Historical Society of Harford County in Bel Air, MD for tombstone image and further cemetery details. Also, *Harford Historical Bulletin* No. 74 (Fall 1997), page 29, contains this information: "Still existing on the island is a solitary grave stone marker dating from 1855. The inscription tells the story of two brothers, Captains Elijah and James Williams, who were lost in a snowstorm near Pooles Island and died, perhaps searching for the welcoming glow of the lighthouse. Elijah's body washed up on shore the following summer, and was presumably buried by the light keeper; James' body was never found. Both men were in their mid-twenties. The inscription reads: 'No friendly hand did close their eyes, They saw no fear [tear], they heard no sighs; But in these [the] waves they lost their breath, And they endured a watry death.' " [Corrections in brackets from government survey]

Williams, Capt. Elijah, lost in snowstorm 24 Feb 1855, age 24, body found 14 Jun 1855

Williams, Capt. James, his brother, lost at same time, age 26, body has not been found

WILLIAMS – NEILSON CEMETERY
(PRIESTFORD CEMETERY)

Tombstones copied by Henry C. Peden, Jr. and photographed by Jack L. Shagena, Jr. on 23 April 2010, supplemented with information written in the notebook of J. Crawford Neilson in 1899. A copy of his notes are microfilmed at the Maryland Historical Society. The cemetery is located about 100 yards south of the house on the farm at 830 Priestford Road. It is enclosed within an electric fence. [Information in brackets below was added by Henry C. Peden, Jr. in 2015.]

Keighler, Rosa Neilson, 15 Mar 1848 - 17 Dec 1913

Neilson, Rosa Williams, wife of J. Crawford, 27 Nov 1818 - 14 Feb 1904 [Her obituary in *The Aegis and Intelligencer* newspaper on 19 Feb 1904 stated she was the widow of J. Crawford Neilson and she died 14 Feb 1904, aged 85, at her home on Deer Creek, daughter of James W. Williams and Hannah Stump, and 1st cousin of Henry W. Archer and Gen. Herman Stump. Her children were Gen. Charles Neilson, Albert Neilson, and Rosa Keighler.]

Neilson, J. [James] Crawford [architect], 14 Oct 1816 - 18 Dec 1900 [His obituary in *The Aegis and Intelligencer* on 21 Dec 1899 stated his family was one of the oldest of South America, but the present generation was born in this country. Crawford was a civil engineer and architect who formed a co-partnership under the name of Niernsey and Neilson [the obituary misspelled Niernsey as Niermey] and designed many buildings (and residences) in Baltimore City and for the U. S. Government. It also stated he was interred in the private burying ground on the home place at Priestford.]

Neilson, James, died 27 Jun 1845, age 4 months

Neilson, Virginia P. [Pendleton], 22 Apr 1846 - 22 Dec 1848

Backer, Edwin A. L., born 15[?] Dec 1845 [marker broken], died 25 Jun 1847 [J. Crawford Neilson made these entries in his 1899 notebook: "Edwd. B. Liot Backer (Demarara) – Son of Mrs. M. J. Neilson – Liot Backer infant 1847"]

"Mammy Jane" [Clarke], died 19 Apr 1874, age 85 [slave and nurse of Rosa Neilson]

Williams, Edwin, 20 Dec 1848 - 14 Apr 1865 [son of James A. and Ruth Williams]

Williams, James A., 14 Apr 1823 - 4 Apr 1849 [son of James W. Williams, 1792-1842]

Williams, James W., 22 Sep 1846 - 26[?] Apr 1849

Williams, Hannah C. [Stump], 18 Jul 1796 - 7 May 1858 [wife of James W. Williams]

Williams, James W., 8 Oct 1792 - 2 Dec 1842 [first person interred in this cemetery]

Williams, James W., aged 11 years, 4 months, --[?] days [no date] [son of James A. Williams]

Williams, Rosa, 1 Mar 184-[?] - 17 Jun 18—[?] [marker illegible; this burial was not listed in J. Crawford Neilson's Notebook in 1899.]

Buried here, according to J. Crawford Neilson in 1899:

Neilson, Mrs. Albert ("Louisa G. Wright"), died 1893

Neilson, Rosa (infant daughter of Charles Neilson), died 1886

Keighler, John Chickley (husband of Rosa Neilson, Jr.), died 1890

Animals (horses and dogs) also buried in this cemetery:

Carlo, 1847-1860	Shepherd, 1883-1900
Black Jack, 1860-1868	Laddie, 1889-1905
Harford, 1862-1894	B. I. F., 1902-1904
Schneider, 1871-1885	

WILSON CEMETERY

This cemetery is located on the west side of Glenville Road on Windmill Hill Farm that was purchased by in 1946 by the father of Peter Jay who presently owns the property. An informative article about the cemetery, titled "In Memoriam," was written by Mr. Jay and printed in the *Sunday Sun* on 4 Apr 1993. He noted that the cemetery is situated on a little hill between his house and the barn. There are also several unmarked stones, but those with markers, copied by unidentified copyists years ago, are as follows:

Wilson, Charlotte, died 4 Feb 1871, age 92

Wilson, George H., died 28 Apr 1834, age 42

Wilson, Elizabeth, died 14 Jul 1829, age 32 years and 5 days

Wilson, William, died 22 Sep 1806 in his 64th year

Wilson, Ruth, consort of W. Wilson, died 1850, age 98

Churchman, Mary [no dates]

Barnes, Mrs. Ann, consort of John Barnes, died 11 Oct 1844 in her 57th year

WILSON GRAVE SITE

The Harford County death certificate of Mary Wilson, daughter of Robert Wilson and Frances Berry, natives of Pennsylvania, indicated this African American infant was stillborn on 13 Jan 1929 and was buried at their home at Rocks in Harford County by her father on 15 Jan 1929.

WILSON GRAVE SITE
An unnamed African American girl, the daughter of John Wilson and Frances Monk, was stillborn on 30 Mar 1932 and buried by her father on "own ground" in Havre de Grace as reported by Dr. Charles J. Foley on her death certificate.

WORTHINGTON(?) CEMETERY
In 2005 John Lamb, of Darlington, now deceased, informed Henry C. Peden, Jr. about three old tombstones on Silver Road in the Shuresville area. The markers were at one time in what is now an orchard at the south of the bend in Silver Road that leads to Camp Ramblewood. In 2005 the markers were in the basement of a house at 2511 Silver Road and Mr. Lamb copied the inscriptions as follows:

S. H. W., died 7 Dec 1857, age 28
W. G. W., died 9 Dec 1857, age 28
L. H. W. [illegible]

It is known that James C. Worthington purchased land from William Worthington (1819-1859) in this area in 1844 (Land Records WSF 113:10). William was also quite active in the underground railroad. It is not yet known if these markers belonged to the Worthington family, or if they pertained to a white or black family. Research thus far has yet to reveal any Worthingtons with the above initials.

WRIGHT CEMETERY
The burial plot at *Wright's Prospect*, as related by C. Milton Wright on 25 Jan 1970, "was in the corner of the orchard at the edge of the woods. This was located at the end of the original lane, not the present lane. It was about 200 feet north of the barn on the tract which Caleb Wright sold to John C. Robinson. It had several graves, probably 8 or 10, marked by common upright fields tones with head and foot markers. It

cannot be recalled whether the stones had any inscription on them. The plot was intact as late as 1910-1915. Daddy remembers the plot well – walking past it on many occasions and recalls seeing the many markers standing in rows. The grave stones were removed during the ownership of John W. Hitchcock and the field cultivated. It was said that the grave stones were moved and piled up in the adjoining woods. The probable graves were those of:" [See the listing below with comments in brackets added by Henry C. Peden, Jr. in 2015.]

Wright, John, Sr., and two wives:

Wright, Maacha [sic] Lowe, died 1826

Wright, Margaret Wilgis
[Someone later wrote "Buried at West Liberty"]

Wright, John, Jr. and wife:

Wright, Agnes Gordon
[Someone later wrote "Buried at West Liberty"]

Children of Caleb Wright:

[Caleb J. Wright married Elizabeth Gilbert in 1825 and they are buried at Ayres Chapel Church.]

Wright, Elizabeth Ann, 6 May 1826 – 19 Sep 1826

Wright, Mary Ann, 18 May 1837 – Aug 1845 (died of diphtheria)

Wright, Joshua Benton, 4 Dec 1838 – 4 Dec 1845 (died of diphtheria)

Wright, Eleanor B., 4 Sep 1840 – 24 Feb 1862

WRIGHT CEMETERY

"Wright Family Notes," by Anna Lee Kirkwood Smith circa 1970s, contained "Information from William N. Wright, age 77, son of William, son of Joshua W., son of William and Amelia, in a visit to his home on August 16, 1975." Amelia Smithson, born circa 1789, was born on the farm on which William Wright is now (1975) living on Telegraph Road near St. Paul's United Methodist Church. Amelia married William Wright in 1804 and they eventually settled on the tract called *Amos' and Myers' Puzzle*. "In the side yard of the property is the private burial ground with a single tall monument. Apple trees [1975] are growing over the older part of the cemetery, but the area is mowed and well kept. On the monument there is only an inscription for William Wright and the two children of John Wesley Wright. Although Amelia left $25 in her will for the erection of the monument, her name is not inscribed." Those persons buried in this cemetery were reported to be as follows. [Information in brackets below was added by Henry C. Peden Jr. in 2015.]

Smithson, Daniel, died 1798 (father of Amelia)

Smithson, Susannah Taylor, 2nd wife (mother of Amelia)
[*Thomas Smithson (1675-1732) of Baltimore County, Maryland and His Descendants*, by Diane Dieterle (1993), page 26, states Susannah Taylor was born in 1753, married Daniel Smithson (1734 – 22 Feb 1798) and died on 7 Oct 1820. Both are buried on the Wright property, Harford Co.]

Wright, William, died 1853

Wright, Amelia, died 1858

Slater, Johanna Wright, died ---- (daughter of William and Amelia)

3 or 4 infants of William and Amelia Wright (there were small stones marked "infant")

2 grandchildren of William and Amelia Wright (the children of John Wesley Wright and his 1st wife Mary Peters)

Wright, William ---- [no dates] (listing stated he was son of William and Amelia and was first buried here, but later removed to Bethel Cemetery) [Bethel Presbyterian Church Cemetery Records state that William Wright, son of William Wright and Amelia Smithson, was born 22 Apr 1826, died 25 Nov 1864 and was buried in Row 7. It did not state that he had been re-interred from the Wright family cemetery.]

INDEX

Dallam, Frances S. 16
Dallam, Francis J. 16
Dallam, Frederick O. 17
Dallam, Josias W. 16
Dallam, Josias W. 17
Dallam, Philip R. 16
Dallam, Sarah 16
Dallam, Sarah P. 16
Dallam, William M. 16
Davidge, John 17
Davidge, Onner H. 18
Davidge, Stewart 18
Davidge, W. H. S. 17
Day, Goldsmith 18, 21
Day, John W. 18, 21
Day, Mary S. 18
De La Porte, Claudius 18
De La Porte, Elizabeth 18
De La Porte, Peter F. 18
Deaver, Aquila 19
Dennison, Araminta 8
Dennison, Lydia E. 8
Denny. Lucy 49
Dever, Elizabeth 87
Dever, John H. 82
Dever, Robert 87
Dicory, Mr. 53
Doran, Edward 19
Doran, Hugh 19
Doran, Margaret 66
Doran, Patrick 19
Dorney, A. M. 20
Dorney, Albert 20
Dorney, Ella L. 20
Dorney, Emlin W. 20
Dorney, George W. 20
Dorney, Ida M. 20
Dorney, Lizzie J. 20
Dorney, Mary 20

Dorney, Thomas 20
Dorsey, Ann, 21
Dorsey, Henry 75, 76
Dorsey, Louisa 96
Dove, Marmaduke P. 22
Dove, Martha G. 23
Dove, Thomas W. 22
Dove, William G. 22
Durbin, Ella J. 68
Durbin, Nathaniel 68
Durbin, Stephen 68
Dutton, Susannah 47
Ecoff, Hannah 90
Enlows, James 23
Enlows, James Jr. 23
Enlows, Prudence 23
Enlows, Rebecca 23
Enlows, Temperance 23
Evans, Hannah S. 86
Evans, L. H. 86
Evans, Rachel S. 86
Farmer, Elizabeth 24
Farmer, Gregory Jr. 24
Farmer, Gregory Sr. 24
Farmer, Rachel E. 24
Farmer, Samuel 24
Farmer, Sarah H. 24
Farnandis, Henry D. 40
Farnandis, Mary D. 76
Fletcher, Albert 5
Fletcher, Mary 5
Fletcher, Samuel 5
Flint, Julia A. 8
Ford, Martha N. 33
Forwood, Eliza 79
Fressonjat, Phillip 58
Fulwiler, Frances S., 66
Gallup, Annie M. 26
Gallup, Charles 25

Osborn, Mary 28
Osborn, Susanna 46
Owens, ---- 50
Paca, John 54
Parker, Carrie 52
Parker, Edward 51
Parker, Henry 52
Parker, Joseph 52
Parker, Joseph C. 51
Parker, Lucy 51
Parker, Margery 52
Parker, Nancy G. 51
Parker, Norman 52
Parker, Sarah H. 51
Paul, Martha G. 22, 23
Pearce, ---- 53
Peters, Mary 104
Phillips, James 54
Phillips, James 73
Phillips, James Jr. 54
Phillips, John P. 54
Phillips, Martha 54, 73
Phillips, William P. 54
Pinion, Susie 71
Platt, ---- 54
Poteet, Corbin 55
Poteet, Elizabeth T. 54, 55
Poteet, James 55
Price, David E. 84
Price, Elizabeth 55
Price, Grace 84
Price, John H. 84
Price, Margaret G. 84
Price, Mary 84
Price, William 55
Pringle, Catharine 56
Pringle, Eliza 55, 56
Pringle, Mark 55, 56
Pyle, Ralph 56

Pyle, Samuel 56
Pyle, Sarah 56
Ramsay, Nathan 74
Ramsly, Henry 73
Raphel, Etienne 57, 58
Raphel, Henrietta 58
Raphel, Jane E. 57, 58
Raphel, Maria E. 58
Raphel, Stephanie 58
Raphel, Stephen 57, 58
Raphel, Stephen J. 57, 58
Reasin, Hannah E. 49
Reasin, William D. 59
Reasin, William H. 49
Reed, C. C. E. J. 49
Reed, Lillie E. 8
Richardson, John 70
Richardson, Minnie 68
Riegel, Carrie T. 83
Riegel, Jacob 83
Rigdon, Charles 14
Rigdon, Elen(?) 59
Rigdon, William 59
Ringgold, John H. 9
Ritchie, Jane 84
Roach, Henrietta 37
Roberts, Ellen 42
Rodgers, Catharine 59
Rodgers, Elijah B. 59
Rodgers, Rowland 59
Rodgers, Sarah J. 59
Ruff, Elizabeth 49
Ruff, Octavian H. 50
Rumsey, Benjamin 60
Rumsey, Caroline B. 60
Rumsey, John 60, 69
Rumsey, Mary H. 60
Rutland, Mary 63
Rutledge, Abraham 61, 62

Stokes, Joseph 79
Stump, Ann 81
Stump, Ann K. 82
Stump, Augustine H. 83
Stump, Cassandra 84, 87
Stump, Duckett 81
Stump, Elizabeth 87
Stump, Frederick 82
Stump, Hannah 86, 87
Stump, Henry 81, 86
Stump, Henry A. 83
Stump, Henry C. 82
Stump, Henry II 86
Stump, Henry III 87
Stump, Herman 84, 87
Stump, James B. 85
Stump, Jane 85
Stump, John 83, 84, 86, 87
Stump, John H. 86
Stump, John K. 82
Stump, John W. 85
Stump, Margaret 85
Stump, Margaret A. 85
Stump, Mary A. 82
Stump, Mary B. 84, 85
Stump, Pauline 86
Stump, Rachel 86
Stump, Rachel C. 87
Stump, Reuben 85
Stump, Samuel C. 81
Stump, Sarah B. 84
Stump, Thomas C. 81, 82
Stump, William 81, 85
Stump, William H. 82, 85
Taylor, Ann 33
Taylor, Corbin 33
Taylor, Henry L. 90
Taylor, James 89
Taylor, John 90

Taylor, Joseph 90
Taylor, Mary 41
Taylor, Nancy 33
Taylor, Virginia 90
Taylor, Baby 90
Thomas, James 90
Thomas, Thomas 90
Thomas, William 90, 91
Thompson, Ann 45
Thompson, Harry 70
Thompson, Martha A. 30
Thompson, Mary 40
Thompson, Sarah B. 6
Thompson, William T. 30
Tildon, Henry E. 9
Tildon, Teavre 70
Todd, George 91
Tolly, James W. 91
Tolly, Joseph 91
Trager, John W. 92
Trager, Sarah A. 92
Trager, William 92
Treadway, Daniel 93
Treadway, Ellen B. 3
Treadway, Sarah 93
Treadway, Thomas 92
Tredway, Aquila E. 3
Tredway, Sarah A. 3
Tucker Rebecca 22
Tucker, Elizabeth 23
Turner, Mary K. 55
Turner, Thomas 55
Turner, William 55
Utie, ---- 93
Wakefield, Arthur F. 53
Waltham, Alice A. 95
Waltham, Clement 95
Waltham, T. P. 22
Waltham, Thomas 22

Ward, Jane 90
Ward, Joseph 90, 91
Warfield, Annie 10
Webster, James B. 94
Webster, John Adams 94
Webster, Rachel 94
Webster, Rachel C. 94
Webster, Susan A. 94
Wells, Mary A., 14
Wesley, Jacob 95
West, Nancy 96
Wheeler, Monica 62
Whitaker, Aquila 96
Whitaker, Joshua 96
Whitaker, Martha 96
Whitaker, Ruth H. 96
Whitaker, Susan 96
Whittington, Andrew T. 96
Whittington, Baby 96
Williams, Edwin 99
Williams, Elijah 97
Williams, Hannah C. 99
Williams, James 85
Williams, James 97
Williams, James A. 99
Williams, James W. 99
Williams, Rosa 99
Williams, William 85
Wilson, Baby 101
Wilson, Charlotte 100
Wilson, Christopher 83
Wilson, Elizabeth 100
Wilson, George H. 100
Wilson, Henry S. 83
Wilson, Hetty 83
Wilson, John 101
Wilson, Mary 83, 100
Wilson, Rachel 83
Wilson, Robert 100

Wilson, Ruth 100
Wilson, William 100
Wilson, William 83
Wilson, William H. 83
Wire, Eve, 66
Wise, Daniel 70
Wise, J. Henry 70
Wise, Mary E. 71
Wise, Milton 71
Wise, Thomas 71
Withers, Caroline 38
Wood, Joy 80
Worthington(?) 101
Wright, Agnes G. 102
Wright, Amelia 103, 104
Wright, Caleb J. 102
Wright, Eleanor B. 102
Wright, Elizabeth A. 102
Wright, John Jr. 102
Wright, John Sr. 102
Wright, John W. 103, 104
Wright, Joshua B. 102
Wright, Maacha L. 102
Wright, Margaret W. 102
Wright, Mary A. 102
Wright, William 103, 104
York, John W. 8

www.ingramcontent.com/pod-product-compliance
Lightning Source LLC
Chambersburg PA
CBHW072159270326
41930CB00011B/2485